THE COMPLETE PAPER QUILLING GUIDE

*This Book Includes: Quilling For Beginners +
Quilling Patterns For Beginners*

by Brenda Sanders

Quilling For Beginners

A Step-By-Step Guide to Learn Everything You Need to Know On the Contemporary Techniques, Patterns and Tools of Paper Quilling In a Quick and Easy Way

Quilling Patterns For Beginners

A Complete Guide To Quickly Learn Paper Quilling Techniques with Illustrated Pattern Designs to Create All Your Project Ideas

Quilling For Beginners

A Step-By-Step Guide to Learn Everything You Need to Know On the Contemporary Techniques, Patterns and Tools of Paper Quilling In a Quick and Easy Way

by Brenda Sanders

Disclaimer

All erudition supplied in this book is specified for educational and academic purposes only. The author is not in any way in charge of any outcomes that emerge from using this book. Constructive efforts have been made to render information that is both precise and effective; however, the author is not to be held answerable for the accuracy or use/misuse of this information.

Foreword

I would like to thank you for taking the first step of trusting me and deciding to purchase/read this life-transforming book. Thanks for investing your time and resources on this product.

I can assure you of precise outcomes if you will diligently follow the specific blueprint I lay in the information handbook you are currently checking out. It has transformed lives, and I firmly believe it will equally change your life, too.

All the information I provided in this Do-It-Yourself piece is easy to absorb and practice.

Table of Contents

Introduction

Paper quilling is known as paper filigree. It can be defined as the art of rolling paper, especially when quilling it, folding it into diverse shapes and designs, pasting it on paper, and making a stunning three-dimensional piece of fine art. It is finished using slim portions of shaded papers, folded into a quilling needle, framing an ideal shape, and finally, the shapes are glued together to form objects.

It is an art highly known for its aesthetic purpose and is commonly used in making jewelry, fancy boxes, greeting cards, flowers for decorating walls, and much more. Lately, it has become a popular part of art gallery exhibitions.

The interesting thing is that you don't need to break your pocket to take up this hobby successfully. You need some basic supplies, but others can be improvised until you can afford them all. You could equally make do with some paper around you, cutting them into strips of paper for your project; this is if you can't access already cut paper strips.

The art includes loads of complex designs that could easily get you frustrated if you don't have the right materials or have knowledge of the basic shapes and how to make them. This book will guide you on the basic shape you need to begin with, and the complex shape you need to master. The starting point is the making of coils (closed and open) from where other shapes and designs surface. Once you've successfully learned this, your journey as a paper quiller begins, and with consistency, while trying out new projects, you'll find yourself at a professional level soon enough.

The origin of paper quilling as an art can be traced as far back as the 16th and 17th centuries. It is believed to have been practiced mainly by Italian and French nuns, whose love for decorating religious objects spurred them to find even better ways of doing so whilst saving the little money they had.

They made use of gold-gilded remnants of paper trimmed off in the process of making books, and this resulted in fine-gold quilled works at the time of emergence. This was a beautiful alternative to golden filigree, which was very expensive at that time, and so was not readily available.

The practice found footing in England in the 18th century with the development of paper, which was then accompanied by the use of vellum and parchment. The art soon became the favorite pastime of ladies who were often referred to as the "the ladies of amusement," a term used to point out ladies who had no house duties and equally had no inclination to take up jobs.

They would often make use of their created designs/quilled works to cover screens, tea-caddies, frames, etc. it soon became part of the curriculum in female boarding schools. It was not practiced then by working-class ladies as they saw it as an art of leisure. Eventually, it also sailed its ship into the United States of America, where it temporarily lost its voice to other more ancient hobbies, like knitting, sewing, painting, etc. The craft further gained footings across the Atlantic with the help of colonial masters who moved from countries to countries, their women bringing with them their favorite pastime routine of quilling.

Despite the odds faced centuries before, the art is now a well-celebrated part of the world's creativity, and this is thanks to the ability to learn anything easily via social media and books. The popularity can also be attributed to its usefulness in children and adult craft, making it possible to keep kids creatively busy in schools and at home. And also, providing awesome pieces for decorating the kids' room, making gift-giving special in a different way, thus showing your loved ones how special and unique they are. Starting is pretty easy; as long as you are interested, you're ready to invest the time needed to learn and the basic materials.

There are a variety of ways to give life to your paper quilling ideas; the use of exceptional 3-dimensional designs is currently the way some unique paper crafters prefer to do their job, others prefer simple tilts towards the less-complex designs, preferring to make earrings, pendants, and others. For others, it is better viewed on canvas in art galleries, and yet others prefer the magnificence of museum walls for the exhibition of the work.

Regarding tools, a variety of simple and complex ones are available for purchase in the paper markets. Some, you can do without; others, you can improvise for. Either way, you won't have any issue sourcing for required materials as a beginner. It is equally advisable as a beginner to make do with the basic tools needed to learn, and then, as time goes on, you can further purchase more complex tools.

Paper quilling is a work of art that is finished by cutting paper into long strips and folding and cutting the pieces into various shapes and attaching them together to frame enhancing artistic ideas. When the paper is moved around a plume to make a basic curl shape, and then, attached at the tip, it's basically known as paper quilling; these molded loops are organized to shape improving blossoms, cards and diverse fancy samples like ironwork.

The Importance of Paper Quilling

Paper quilling is exceptionally straightforward brightening craftsmanship that even a fledgling can ace in an hour or two. In spite of the fact that only your creative mind can limit the potential outcomes, the beautiful pieces can be basic or complex relying upon your assurance. Yet, one thing is without a doubt, paper quilling is the ideal art project anybody can begin anytime. Regardless of whether you are only an amateur, you can accomplish the best outcome in the blink of an eye. Moreover, the discipline cost is practically close to nothing, so if, you are hoping to begin it as a relaxation action or a wellspring of salary, paper quilling is one of the most significant artwork you can wander into without the slightest hesitation about putting resources into it, in light of the fact that the ornamental artistry structures can pay ordinarily more than you put in.

Chapter 1: Types of Paper Recommended for Quilling

On the off chance that you are an amateur in this art, it's likely that you may, at one point or another, settle on an off-base decision with regards to the correct sort of paper material to use for a particular sort of work. Be that as it may, it's likewise applicable even to the individuals who appear to be experts in this art.

A few people will in general buy papers in open markets, online shopping centers, or grocery stores, and do the strip cutting without anyone else with either scissors or the convenient paper shredder; and there are other people who simply feel free to get the already-made ones.

This is a fundamental thought to set up before picking a specific paper. This means it has to do with the accessible thickness of the paper as it goes far to influence the external appearance of your completed task/work. For better comprehension of what this implies, here is a breakdown of what the content weight paper strip and the composing weight paper strip are about. Demanding that this will help the assurance of the beginner who thus would be glad to see his/her undertaking come out great without a lot of pressure.

Paper is fundamental in quilling everything, reflected in the title. You could purchase both pre-cut paper strips or genuinely cut the pieces yourself. There are advantages and terrible drawbacks to the two styles of paper strips, with pre-cut paper which is essential and productive anyway, being fairly more exorbitant than DIY paper strips.

Pre-Cut Paper Strips for Quilling

You can purchase quilled paper in a pre-cut structure, saving you time and power from measuring and cutting. Quilling units for juveniles customarily join pre-cut strips.

Making Your Own Paper Strips for Quilling

Through cutting paper strips yourself, you will save money with the pace of time. What is fine is that you may use additional paper you may have from various sources. You will moreover have the opportunity to apply paper that changes in tendency, surface, or models.

The Way to Make Your Personal Paper Strips

There are different strategies to make your own paper strips: mechanical or manual. The mechanical strategy uses a shredder, while the manual system fuses cutting paper with a decreasing device involving a couple of scissors, a sharp edge, or a paper trimmer.

Regardless, when you decide to move the manual course and use scissors, a ruler and pencil will be required to help measure. In case you use a paper trimmer, you will have the choice to stay away from those extra resources.

A shredder can have the alternative to make strips for you quickly, but will no longer have the ideal edges which you will require for your masterpiece. This methodology may also not be prepared for getting you the right width you liked either. Purchasing a shredder for paper quilling can in like manner be difficult. I wouldn't use a shredder to convey strips for paper quilling. It is by and by not a dependable system for creating splendid, solid strips to apply to your quilling pieces.

What Sort of Paper Do I Exploit for Quilling?

Pre-cut strips will ordinarily be available in paper with an appropriate weight. In case you are cutting your own strips, I would urge beginning with paper weighing 120 grams (grams per square meter) as it is valuable for rolling and making shapes. Regardless, you could use something from 80-160 grams for paper quilling.

Other master quillers would suggest that, as a tenderfoot, you can use the precut-paper strip for your first undertaking.

Advantages and Disadvantages in Using the Precut-Paper Strip

At the point when you start your paper quilling works, you will soon notice that getting or requesting precut-paper strips (already-made papers) has a lot of negatives when contrasted with its positives.

A few people might oppose to this, but you realize everybody has his/her preferences as this is mine. Along these lines, you reserve the privilege to oppose, but as a matter of fact, making your paper strip is much better as it opens you to an enormous chance/space to finding out more and more grounds in this specialty.

- **Preferences:**
1. It is efficient. This means the time you would have used in cutting/making your own paper strips will be spared and preserved for other positive use on the task or something else.
2. While utilizing the precut paper-strips, it is exceptionally simple to deal with and situate for potential safekeeping when essential.

3.   The issues of deciding for a paper brand and shading when you are locally sourcing for your quilling materials.

4.   It can likewise make your work neater. This is as indicated by some quilling specialists, they think that because of the way that some of these precut are all around bundled and flawlessly cut, they go further to make your work slick and progressive.

- **Disservices:**

Like the saying goes that everything that has advantages, should most likely have disadvantages. So it goes for the paper quilling precut paper strips.

1.   Initially, when you start, it happens that you have available all you truly need to begin this trip (especially the precut), but you may feel that the already-made papers are anything but difficult to get a hold of, as you would prefer. Be that as it may, that isn't the situation!

2.   When you happen to be in a condition where you can't lay your hands on your favored precut paper shading, surface. and brand, you end up getting abandoned and disappointed with the task. Also, if care isn't taken, you may end up pulling out from this exquisite specialty work, even before you begin.

3.   Another thing that may intrigue you and simultaneously be a source of stress to you is that you don't have the foggiest idea how to cut your paper yourself.

Chapter 2: Basic Shapes and Rolling Paper

Start with Basic Shapes

Start with basic shapes, similar to the roundabout paper curl. Expand upon this fundamental structure as you ace the ability to make a spread of shapes like the paisley, tear, marquis, tulip, or slug. You can crush, squeeze, and manage the moving paper loop's degree until you get the quilled shape of your preference.

Here are some helpful rules for developing the key moved paper loop:

- Add some of the paper into the space of your device, and with your thumb and index finger on both sides of the paper strip, keep it up with even strain as you switch device in reverse or advances.
- At the point when you reach the end of your paper strip, take it off the gadget. Ensure you don't wind it too firmly; else, you could find it a bit dangerous to take it off the device.
- On the off chance that you simply should make a free curl shape, you may allow the paper loop to reach out before getting rid of it from the gadget, yet if you need a tighter loop, don't allow it to harden before you take it off.

Move Beyond the Shapes

Whenever you have made the energizing shapes, cross here and play around with them. You may:

- Use them to embellish a welcome card.
- Make alluring, carefully assembled studs.
- Create outlined fine art to include a scramble of shading and imagination to your dividers.
- Create 3-dimensional figures and miniatures.
- The openings are perpetual!

Building up a bloom is one of the most straightforward quilling activities that will let you get the elements' grip. Simply watch this method:

- Make two flimsy portions of shaded quilling paper to make the focal point of the bloom. Cut a much more extensive strip—double the slenderer strips' width—for the bloom petals.
- Using a quilling needle or toothpick, make a nice move off the slenderer strip. Then paste the end part of the slenderer curled strip.
- Incorporate another slender strip and move it around the main roll. Paste the end of some portion of the strip to make a firmly moving center for the blossom.
- Now, make cuts all close by the more extensive strip half of the strip down its extent. Add the paste to one finish of this strip and move it over the firmly moved blossom center we made in the first step.
- Paste the finish of the greater strip. When the paste is evaporated pleasantly, use your thumb and palms to overlay the petals outward. That's it—your blossom is done!

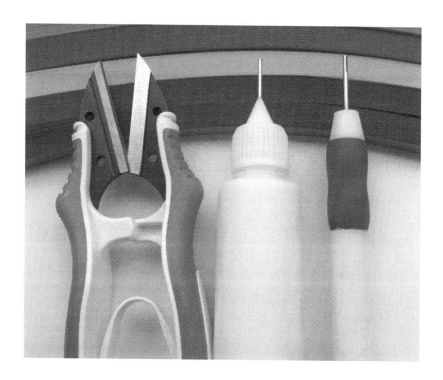

What You Need

- A slotted quilling tools
- Quilling glue in a needle-tip bottle
- Scissors
- Tweezers
- Package of quilling paper strips—for beginners, I recommend ¼-inch wide (it's easy to grip and manipulate); once you've mastered the basic shapes, you may prefer narrower strips. Cut the strips 8½-inches long for this tutorial.

Open and Closed Coils

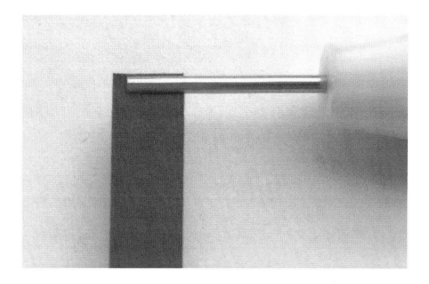

Simple circles are the basis for most other shapes you'll create.

1. Insert paper into the tool

Insert a piece of quilling paper into the slot of your quilling tool; try to line up the paper's edge with the edge of the slot as perfectly as you can. A slotted tool will naturally leave a small crimp in the center of your coil. If you'd like the crimp to be more visible, allow the paper to hang slightly over the edge.

2. Start rolling

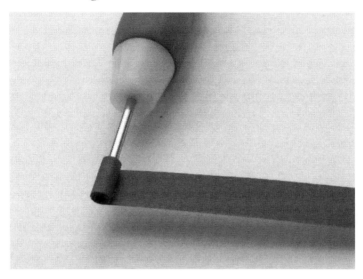

Roll the tool with your dominant hand towards your body or away from it (whichever feels most comfortable) while holding the strip taut with your other hand.

3. Glue it

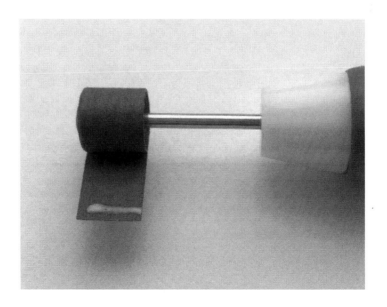

For a closed coil: When you're almost done coiling, place a dab of glue near the end of the strip and roll to complete. You don't want it to expand after you remove it from the tool.

For an open coil: Finish the coil, remove it from the tool, and expand. Once it has fully expanded, add a dab of glue and press the strip down carefully to secure it.

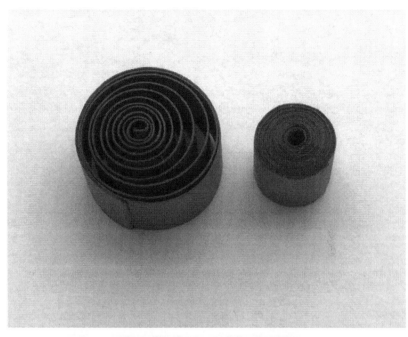

Teardrop

Make an open coil, then place it between the thumb and forefinger of your non-dominant hand. Arrange the inside coils evenly or however you'd like.

With your dominant hand, pinch the paper where you want the point
of the teardrop shape.

27

Teardrop Variations

Basic shapes can be manipulated to create even more shapes. The teardrop is an excellent example of this.

By slightly curving the teardrop around your thumb as you shape it, you can create a subtle shift in form without compromising the center coils. To exaggerate this effect, you can wrap the teardrop around your quilling tool or another cylindrical object.

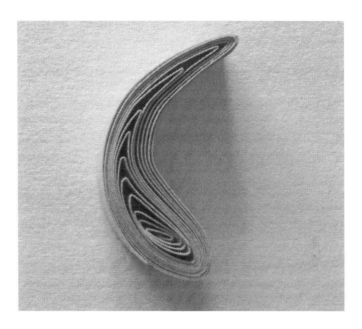

For a more obvious curved shape throughout, press the shape around your quilling tool. From here, you can easily create a paisley shape.

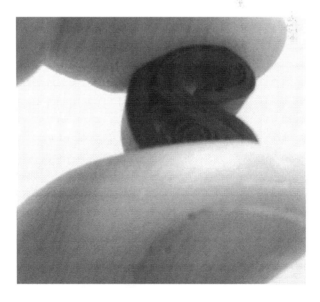

You can curl the shape from the point to the base by rolling it between your fingers.

So many shapes!

Marquis

First, make a teardrop shape, then pinch the opposite end as well.

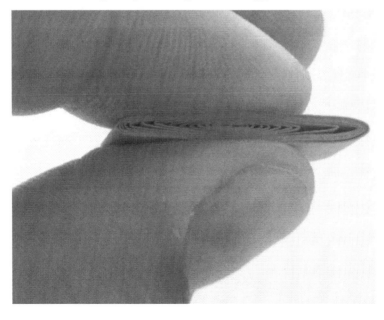

The final shape will be determined by how much you pinch or press the coil together and where you place its center.

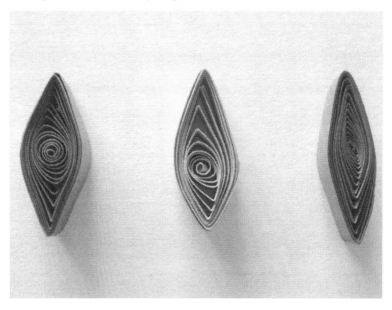

Play around with different placements and pressure to create lots of marquis versions.

Tulip

First, make a marquis shape, then turn the shape on its side and pinch a center peak with your fingers.

Slug

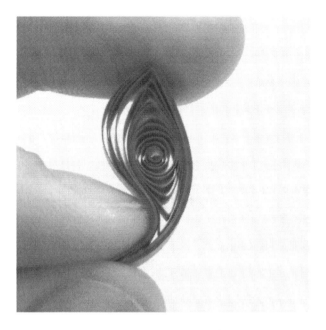

Start with a marquis, then wrap one end around the tip of your finger or a quilling tool.

Do the same to the other end but in the opposite direction. It looks pretty for a slug, doesn't it!

Square or Diamond

Create a marquis shape, then rotate it 90 degrees and pinch both sides again. This will create a diamond shape.

If you want to continue to make a square, gently open up the shape between your fingers.

Square Variations

By playing around with how much of each corner you choose to pinch when creating your square, you can get very different results.

Above left: By applying pressure to the outside corners, you can create a square with a rounded center.

Above center: This was made by completely pressing the open coil together on one side, then opening it up and pinching just the corners on the opposite side.

Above right: This got its unique center by completely pressing down the coil on both turns.

Yet another variation on the square: You can make these by applying pressure to the outside structure with your fingers or the stem of your quilling tool.

Rectangle

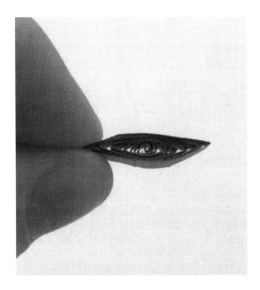

If you can make a square, you can make a rectangle. The difference is in how much you rotate the marquis shape before pinching additional angles.

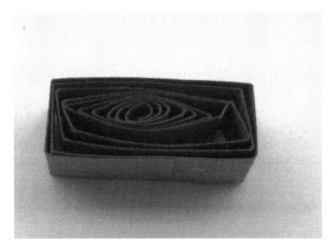

Rotate it only slightly (rather than 90 degrees) before pinching and then open the shape to reveal the perfect rectangle.

Rectangle Variations

Otherwise, you can create a quadrilateral shape by making your four corners at uneven intervals.

This shape is especially useful when you're making quilled paper mosaics, and you need to fill in an odd space.

Semi-Circle

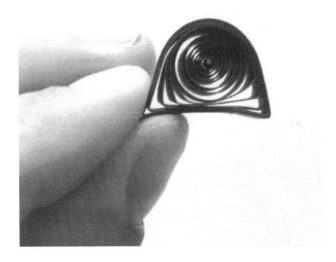

Start with an open coil, then pinch two corners while leaving the paper above them round. You can also do this by pressing an open coil onto a hard surface like a table and carefully sliding your fingers down the sides. Try both methods to see which suits you best.

Curving the shape's straight edge will allow you to turn a semi-circle into more of a crescent moon shape.

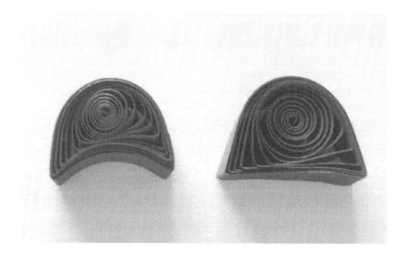

Triangle

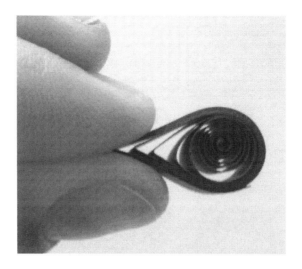

Make a teardrop shape, then pinch two additional angles using either your fingers or the tabletop method.

Once again, try both to see what works best for you.

Triangle Variation

To create a shape that resembles a shark fin, press in two sides of your triangle and leave the third side flat.

Arrow

Make a teardrop, then pull the center down towards the base and hold it in place with your fingers.

Using the long side of the slotted needle, press down deeply into the base.

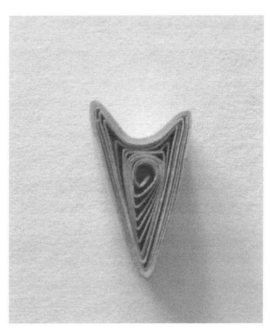

Release the tool and smooth the curve out with your fingers to shape.

Arrowhead

Beginning with a teardrop shape, hold the pointed end in your non-dominant hand and pinch the base end into a tight point.

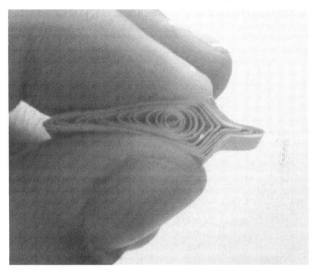

Without letting go, slide your fingers down to meet the fingers of your opposite hand to create the side angles

Heart

Once again, begin with a teardrop. Press in the shape's base by using the point of your quilling tool to make a small indentation.

Release the tool and carefully press in each side of the heart to complete the center crease.

Pentagon and Star

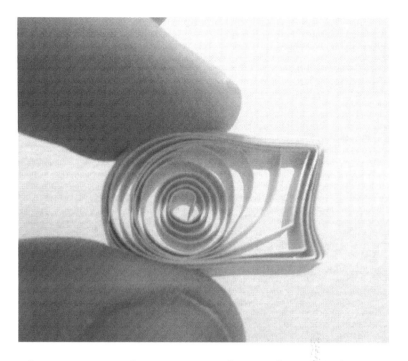

To make a pentagon, first, create an elongated semi-circle, as shown above.

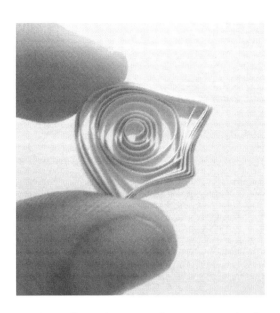

Pinch the center of the flat side using the same method you used when making the tulip shape; this is the peak of your pentagon.

Keeping the peak in the center, square off the bottom with two equal pinches on either side.

To turn the pentagon into a star, press inward on each flat surface with your fingers or a quilling tool and then further refine each angle into peaks.

Holly Leaf

This shape is far and away from the most difficult to create. For sanity's sake, you'll want to become comfortable making all of the other shapes before attempting this one!

Begin by making a marquis. Insert a set of tweezers into the shape; try to grip only about a third of the inside coil.

Keeping the grip with your tweezers, turn the marquis as needed and pinch a small point on either side of each peak.

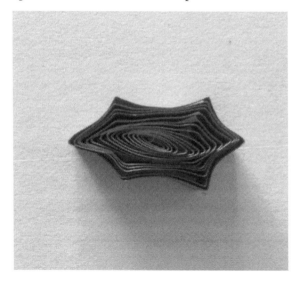

You could also make the holly leaf by first making a square, adding a point to each end, and then shaping all the angles into peaks. I find the tweezer method easier, but try both ways to see which gives you better results.

Chapter 3: Tools and Material

Some have kits, some have drawers, and some have an entire room dedicated to their art and craft supplies. It is best to start quilling with a kit. While it is satisfying to hoard materials, you might end up feeling distracted and overwhelmed by the number of paper strips and tools at your disposal—Master a few tools and the basic techniques first before trying out more materials.

Quilling kits for beginners are readily available in many online quilling supply stores. Most of the kits contain a pack of precut quilling paper and a slotted tool. Some have boards and combs. Many kits also have non-specialty tools (Think of glue, tweezers, and pins).

If you want to fill your quilling kit, you must prepare your own storage box first. You can either buy or improvise. Next, you should shop online for specialty tools. Visit your school supply store for the basic art and craft supplies. Also, search your home for some alternative and additional shaping tools.

Specialty Tools

Specialty tools are made specifically for art—in this case, quilling. They are designed in such a way that they provide convenience to a craft-maker. Right now, some tools are labeled according to the level of expertise of the intended users. You should pick tools that are tagged for beginners. Below are the quilling tools that you should know.

Slotted Tool

The slotted tool is the best friend of every beginner in quilling. This is primarily for making coils. It has two parts: the handle and the needle. The needle part is metal, at least 1/2-inch long, and has a slit where you will place the tip of your paper strip. The said slit makes rolling easier, but it leaves a tiny crimp in the middle of your paper. Its handle may be made from plastic or wood. Most slotted tools have a cylindrical handle. Some may be etched or molded differently. The length of the handle and needles varies from one model to another.

Needle Tool

The needle tool, also known as the needle form, is also intended for making coils. Unlike the slotted tool, though, this one does not have a slit in its needle part, which results in a crimp-less coil. It is best to master the slotted tool first, followed by the needle tool, and then the quilling comb.

Quilling Coach

Quilling coach is a flat plastic board made to help keep the paper strips in place as you roll it using the slotted tool. It is also used to ensure that the edges of your coils are even. This tool has a circular head and a handle. Its head features circles of different sizes and a hole in the middle where you can insert the slotted tool's needle. Most quilling coaches are made from either colored or transparent plastic.

Circle Sizer/Mold Board

A circle sizer is also intended to help you make coils of the same size. Unlike a quilling coach, though, you need to remove your rolled paper strip from the needle tool and then place it on the circle sizer. There are two types of circle sizer: the ruler type and the board type. The ruler type, which may be made from plastic, looks like a typical ruler but bigger and with circular holes of different sizes in the middle part. You are going to put your rolled paper strips in the holes. The board type may be made from either plastic or wood. Aside from circles, the board type may feature molding holes for square, triangle, heart, oval, leaf and other shapes. This one is sometimes referred to as the quilling moldboard.

Quilling Comb

A quilling comb, also known as an onion holder, looks like the one you use for your hair, except that the metallic teeth are longer and the handle is shorter in the former. Compared to the slotted tool, you can form various shapes and patterns with this instrument.

Crimper Tool

As its name suggests, the crimper tool helps you make uniformly crimped paper strips. This is a great time and energy saver as you do not need to fold the paper strips by hand alone.

Quilling Border Buddy

The slotted tool can only help in making circular coils. A quilling border buddy is an answer to the slotted tool's limitation. You can mold your paper strips with the quilling border buddy to form squares or triangles of different sizes. You can also make bigger circles with this tool.

Additionally, you may use this to make borders, which you can fill with smaller paper rings later on. This tool is either wood- or plastic-made.

There are other specialty tools made for quilling, but most of them are for molding. You can opt for the more complex molders later. For now, you should try alternatives molders that you can easily find in your home.

Alternatives

Resourcefulness is one of the attributes of every craft-maker. Apart from cutting their quilling paper strips, some quillers go as far as making their versions of the slotted tool. You do not have to do that. However, it pays to use the alternatives as you wait for your slotted tool and precut quilling paper to arrive. Or, you may also use them alongside the specialty tools to form rings of different sizes.

Toothpicks

The diameter of a standard toothpick is close to that of a slotted tool's needle. Toothpicks are quite easy to break, but practicing your rolls with them can help you learn how to gently roll your paper strips.

Pencils and Pens

Using pencils and pens for your rolls will leave behind noticeable holes in your paper coils. This does not have to be a drawback. You can mix and match coils whose holes are of different sizes for your artworks.

Knitting Needles

The use of knitting needles as an alternative quilling tool is similar to that of pencils and pens. Knitting needles are just a bit lighter. However, if no one likes knitting in your home, finding these tools entails additional work. You should just focus on things that are readily available in your house.

Combs

Your regular combs will work fine as quilling combs. Get some of the combs you rarely use but still look neat. Wash and brush them first before you use them for quilling. Once you decide to use them for quilling, do not reuse them for combing your hair.

Lids

Small lids can serve as additional tools to a quilling border buddy. You can scour your kitchen for old bottles and jars. Get the lids, wash them, and leave them to dry. You can wrap your paper strips around a lid to mold them.

Bottles, containers, chopsticks, or even woodblocks may be used for molding and making coils. Just remember to clean or smoothen the items you intend to use for quilling. You do not want to stain your paper strips with sauces from the old bottles, do you?

Basics

Quilling is not just about shaping paper strips. It also involves other steps, such as measuring, tracing, cutting, gluing, and pinching. For the other steps, you should include pencils and rulers, as well as the following supplies in your quilling kit:

- **Cutting Tools**

Besides investing in good scissors exclusive for quilling, it pays to have a sharp cutter and a self-healing mat. You should add a thread snipper in your kit as well. Although a thread snipper is mainly used for sewing, it can also cut paper quickly and comfortably. It also pays to have a cuticle nipper in your kit as you can use it to cut some uneven parts in your quilled paper strips. Additionally, you may use it to get rid of visible dried glue.

- **Adhesives**

Forget the glue gun for quilling. Needle-tip craft glue is more appropriate. The heat from a glue gun may damage your quilling paper. With craft glue, there would be not much of a problem. Another advantage of this adhesive is its narrow opening, which results in easy application to thin paper strips.

- **Tweezers**

Have at least two pairs of tweezers in your quilling kit. This will help you hold your coils without unraveling or warping them and place your delicate paper strips into narrow spaces.

- **Pins and Tacks**

You can have different pins in your quilling kit. You may choose from the following type: glass headpins, plastic headpins, ballpoint pins, eye pins, silk pins, quilting pins, and T pins. You will use the pins as guards to your paper coils to prevent them from unraveling on the board. You may also use a pin to unclog your needle-tip craft glue. Have a box of tacks as well.

- **Board**

Boards are for the background of some quilled artworks. You are going to use corkboards for practices as well. In the meantime, you may resort to cardboard. Invest in sturdier boards once you have mastered the basics of quilling. Some quilled projects call for additional tools and supplies. Nevertheless, the abovementioned materials are the things you are most likely to work on within most of your practices and projects. Do not forget to experiment with some of the home objects that you may use for rolling and molding.

Chapter 4: Quilling Basics and Tips for Beginners

As a beginner quilter or even as an expert/professional whose interest is to survive in the craft of quilling without much stress, here are few tips that could help you actualize this. They include.

Using a Background Platform that is Colored

If you use a quilling background, attractively laden with colors, it will help boost the sight impression and improve your craftwork's attention after completion and while on display. If the kind of background paper you are using is void of color or colors, say a plain white sheet, you can easily give the paper any color of your choice, and that's it; you've just made one for yourself.

Use Paper Strip (Shredder)

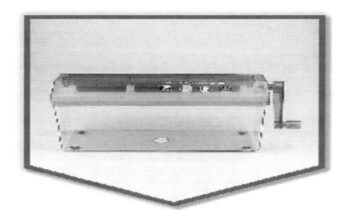

A shredder in paper quilling is a box-like tool normally made of plastic materials with a winding handle. The paper to be threaded is placed neatly in the opened allowable part of the box, and the handle is wind. It is the manual paper stripping method.

Using the scissors to do your quilling process could be cumbersome and tiring sometimes. Subsequently, it is suggested that you opt for the thread sniper or slicer. In this way, you save some time and get near-perfect quilled paperwork free from glue attachments.

However, it is not to say that the scissors aren't a good companion in this business. The scissor can still be effectively used in the absence of any other better alternative.

Use the Needle Before the Comb

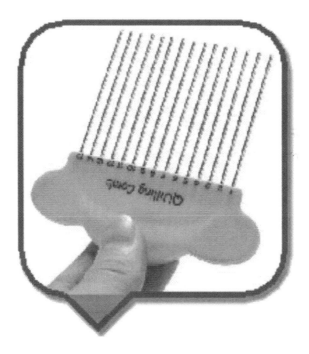

In this craft, the experience pays quite a lot! Some persons find the quilling comb quite difficult to use in the first place. Using the quilling needle tool first before applying the quilling comb would help save a lot, both time and energy, and help keep the middle of your rolled coil in check.

Learn to Roll Two Strips Together

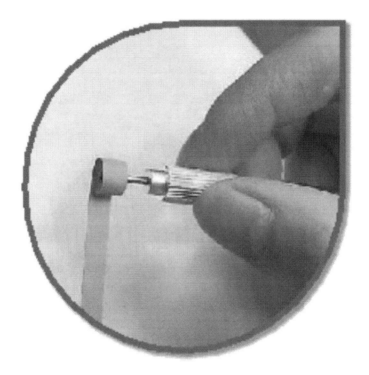

As you continue to grow in this craft experience, you will come to discover that rolling up just a single paper strip could lead to weariness. Still, it is advisable for you and the strip to always join at least two strips together before taking a manual hand roll.

Get a Quilling Sponge

The quilling sponge is more or less like a holding container that helps to hold the glue bottle while working. It is to prevent unsolicited glue/gum spillage on a given job or project, as the glue bottle or container is normally placed or turned with its tip facing downwards on the sponge for easy access and quick application. The sponge also serves as a tool for cleaning up unwanted glue. Particularly those that are on the fingers and palms, in addition to spillovers, if any.

Rolling Using a Slotted Tool

This technique lets you create coils out of your quilling paper strips. Coils are present in most quilt creations, so it only fits to know how to make them. To learn how to roll properly, grab a paper strip and your slotted tool. Keep your needle-tip craft glue nearby and follow the steps below:

1. Hold the slotted tool using your dominant hand while the paper strip is in your other hand.
2. Insert the tip of your paper strip into the slit of your slotted tool's needle.
3. Hold the paper strip with your non-dominant hand's thumb and index finger.
4. Start rolling the slotted tool. It is the right way. Do not wrap the paper strip around the slotted tool's needle.
5. You may roll the paper strip up to the very end or leave something like a tail.

There are three types of coils you can create with the steps mentioned above. These are: open, closed and tight.

To make an open coil, gently remove the rolled paper strip from the slotted tool and put it down right away.

To make a closed coil, gently remove the rolled paper strip from the slotted tool, let it loosen but apply a small amount of glue at the end of the paper strip.

To make a tight coil, gently remove the rolled paper strip from the slotted tool and hold it lightly for 20 seconds. Apply glue at the end of the paper strip.

If you want your coils to be of similar size, make sure that the paper strips you use are also of the same size. Additionally, use your circle sizer ruler or board to measure your coils.

Create as many coils as you can until you master rolling with your slotted tool. Do not throw your coils right away, though. No matter how displeasing they might seem, you can use them to try forming the basic shapes and learning how to insert small coils into big ones later.

You'd be surprised that you can master this technique in an hour or two. You should be warned, though. Rolling paper strips continuously may lead to cramps. To prevent this, relax your grip on your slotted tool and paper strip. Stretch and let your fingers rest every so often. You might want to consider holding a cloth or padding between your dominant hand and the slotted tool.

Rolling Using a Needle Tool, Toothpick, or Any Other Alternative

Rolling using a needle tool, toothpick, or any other alternative to the slotted tool is a little bit harder because of the lack of slit where you can place one end of your paper strip. Although tricky, this technique does not leave behind a crimp in the middle of your coil, which usually happens when you use the slotted tool.

To start, keep your fingers a little bit moist and follow the steps below:

1. Use your dominant hand to hold your tool while your other hand is for the paper strip. You may add a quilling coach to your needle tool.
2. Curve the end of the paper strip around your tool. Do this near the tip of the tool for easy and speedy removal of coils later.
3. Gently press the end of the paper strip attached to your tool to keep it in place.
4. Start rolling your tool.

To create the three types of coils using a needle tool, toothpick, or any other alternative, follow through the same steps as those mentioned for rolling with a slotted tool. When you are done mastering the art of making coils, go to a whole new level by transforming your coils into basic quilling shapes. You can do this by hand alone. The following are some of the basic quilling shapes you can create with your paper coils.

Practice making basic shapes as many times as you want. Experiment with wider and narrower paper strips, as well as with longer and shorter paper strips. You can also try modifying the techniques bit by bit

- **Teardrop**

To make a teardrop-shaped paper strip, pinch one part of your coil. Apply glue at the end.

- **Eye**

Pinch two opposite ends of your coil. Make sure they are equally molded on each side. Glue the loose end of your coil.

- **Leaf**

The leaf-shaped coil is similar to the eye. You also have to pinch two opposite parts of your coil. After that, push the pinched parts towards each other. Do not forget to apply glue at the other end.

- **Petal**

To create a petal-shaped coil, you should also pinch two opposite parts of your coil. However, one of the pinched parts should be bigger than the other.

Practice making these basic shapes as many times as you want. Experiment with wider and narrower paper strips, as well as with longer and shorter paper strips. You can also try modifying the techniques bit by bit.

Rolling Using a Border Buddy or Any of Its Alternatives

Some quilling border buddies have handles, so learning how to use them is easier. However, some do not have any handle at all. You have no other option but to hold the body of the border buddy. But this could be an advantage. You will be trained to use the border buddy and lids, small bottles, or any other item used as a molder.

The steps for rolling a paper strip using a border buddy or any of its alternatives are similar to rolling using a needle tool unless your molder is not round, oblong, or oval. Always start with round border buddies. Try creating big coils of different sizes. Once you are done with the round ones, proceed with the triangle and square border buddies. When you use a lid, make sure your paper strip is narrower. Otherwise, you will lead up with a coil full of crimps on the edges. Below are the steps in using a border buddy or any other molder for that matter:

1. Use your dominant hand to hold the molder while the other hand is for your paper strip.

2. Put one end of your paper strip into the molder. Press it with your thumb to keep it in place.

3. Start twisting your molder slowly but guide your paper strip using your non-dominant hand's thumb and index finger. If your molder has one or more corners, press your paper strip in those corners.

4. After the first roll, apply glue to the end of your paper strip that is affixed to your molder.

5. Continue rolling until you achieve your desired thickness. You may or may not leave something like the tail of your coil.

If you are going to make a closed coil, do not remove your paper strip from the molder right away. Apply glue at the other end of your paper strip while it is still on the molder. After that, remove your paper strip and hold it for 20 seconds (or until the glued end is not likely to slide) to maintain its shape.

Create coils of different colors, shapes, sizes, widths, and lengths. Try out various plastic and glass bottles, jars, and other containers. Use wood blocks to make big squares, rectangles, or triangles. You may transform your coils into other shapes by pinching them or just leave them as they are.

Gluing Coils Together

Gluing coils are made easy and less messy with needle-tip craft glue. But for your practices, it might be a waste to use such glue right away. As an alternative, you may use regular glue and a pin.

You are going to use the glue to join coils together. For now, you can glue the different coils you just created. Do not obsess about forming patterns in the meantime. Below are the steps in applying regular glue using a pin.

1. Prepare your tweezers, cuticle nipper, and a piece of scrap paper.
2. Squeeze a little amount of glue to the piece of paper. Close your glue to keep it from drying.
3. After that, get a bit of glue using your pin and spread it to one side of the coil. You may use your hands to hold big coils, but you should use tweezers for the small ones.
4. Get another coil and affix it to the glued part of one coil. Hold it together for at least 20 seconds or until the glue dries.

Practice gluing coils that are of the same width. Use your cuticle nipper to get rid of dried glue or to cut some uneven parts.

Gluing Coils on a Medium

One of the simplest quilled artworks you can make is card designs. You do not need to glue coils together for this. You can attach the coils directly to your card or any other medium. For this, you need to put a small amount of glue at the bottom of your coils and glue it to paper. Try gluing coils of different shapes individually. After that, try to put coils together. To do this, follow the steps for gluing coils together first. Apply glue to the bottom of your adjoined coils and affix it to your paper.

Inserting Small Coils into Big Coils

One of the toughest steps in creating a quilled artwork is inserting small coils into big ones. To help you stay sane throughout the entire process, get your two tweezers and a handkerchief for your sweaty hands. Prepare your big coils and small coils as well. Below are the steps in inserting small coils:

1. Glue your big coils on paper. Do not worry about forming figures or patterns for now. Just glue them.
2. Next, apply glue to the bottom and sides of your small coils.
3. After that, use your tweezers to insert the small coils to fill up the big coils' holes. Start inserting the slightly bigger ones first.
4. If there are some noticeable spaces left, make small coils that can fit into those. You may cut the coils you already need to form the small coils.

For the loose and open coils, you can place them beside the big coils. Put a paste to the bottom and sides of the coils. These are going to be linked to the other coils. It is quite tedious to apply glue to the bottom of loose coils, especially if they have tails.

Here is an important reminder when applying glue: It is better to apply a little more than a little less. If you apply a too small amount, your coil may get detached easily. If you apply a little more, you can simply remove the excess dried glue with a cuticle nipper or a pin. A pin works best for the dried glue in the inner parts of the coil. If it is quite difficult to reach, though, it is better to leave the dried glue in peace.

Using a Quilling Comb

There are plenty of elaborate coils you can make with the quilling comb. However, this tool is also complicated to use. You are going to combine weaving and looping when you use the quilling comb. Below are some of the basic shapes you can make with a quilling comb.

- **Petal**

With the quilling comb, you can make paper petals without pinching your coils. There are many petal designs you can form with the quilling comb but below are the steps to make it easier.

- Hold your paper strip using your dominant hand while the quilling comb is at your other hand.
- Fold a tiny part at the end of the paper strip to create a hook.
- Place your paper strip at the back of the quilling comb. Hook it at the bottommost tine of the quilling comb. The tiny folded part should be at the front.

- Pull the other end of the paper strip to the front on the second tine of the quilling comb.
- Apply glue to the tiny folded part of the paper strip.
- Fold the long end of the paper strip and glue it to its tiny folded part. Press it gently.
- Pull the long end to the back of the paper strip again.
- Weave the paper strip to the front on the third tine of the quilling comb.
- Pull the long end down and then fold it to the back of the quilling comb again. Apply glue to the part where the hook was once located.
- Repeat the same steps to the succeeding tines of your quilling comb.
- Keep on looping until the end of your paper strip. If there is an excess, cut it using a thread snipper.

Just like making coils with the slotted tool, you may simply remove your paper strip and let it loosen. You may or may not glue its other end. If you want it to be a tight coil, hold the two ends for at least 20 seconds and then apply glue at the end. Or, you may just hold the one end where the hook was and let the other end loosen.

Chapter 5: Practical Tips to Make Projects Faster

Paper quilling is madly cool, however, in case you're an apprentice, the expectation to absorb information can be steep. Fortunately, knowing a couple of crucial tips and hacks has a significant effect.

Utilize Beautiful Foundations

A prominent white foundation can be diverting and point out every blemish, while a shaded foundation offers marginally less complexity to your quilled shapes and is substantially more sympathetic. It'll assist watchers with seeing precisely what you need them to concentrate on the general perfection of your design.

Pick String Snippers Over Scissors

Picking the correct paper quilling devices is significant, and cumbersome scissors are not your companion in this sensitive art. You're in an ideal situation with a lightweight pair of string snippers. They're suitable for clipping off the glue-bound parts of the snips, and their little size causes them to fit excellently into any quilling tool compartment.

Get an Ideal Center Coiling in Each of Your Coiling

You needn't bother with a needle device to make a flawless coil. Whenever utilized the correct way, an opened equipment can give you the round focus you need without creasing.

One stunt is to continue turning your quilling instrument after you've arrived at the finish of your strip until you feel the device give way. The device tears the little bit of paper that would've been the crease, leaving you with an ideal curl. On the off chance that your quilling device can't confront this sort of turning, you can likewise use a pin or penetrating device to streamline the pleat a while later.

Tear as Opposed to Clipping

Yes, you need to make clean lines and shroud all the creases in your shapes at whatever point conceivable. Be that as it may, now and then there's no place to stow away. On the off chance that you don't care for the vibe of sharp paper creases, you can tear the finish of your quilling strip as opposed to clipping it with scissors. That way, the join will have a milder impact.

Move With, Not Against, the Edge of the Quilling Strip

When quilling paper gets cut, the sharp edge cuts it from above in a descending movement. This makes both of the long sides roll somewhat descending. The impact is insignificant to such an extent that it's difficult to see with the naked eye, yet you can feel it when you run the strip between your fingers. For a progressively flawless curl, move with the bend (the descending arch should look down). It may be somewhat dubious to do this on your initial attempts, and avoiding this progression won't hurt the manner in which your quilled look. Be that as it may, when you begin focusing, doing it alongside these lines turns out to be practically instinctual.

Utilize a Needle Structure Before a Quilling Brush or Comb

Quilling brushes or comb can appear to be difficult and tedious to use. You may feel like they're not worth the effort, however, attempt this tip before you abandon them: first, roll a little curl using a quilling needle tool. At that point, move the coil to your quilling brush and make your shape. This technique needle structure first, quilling brush after should help keep the focal point of your loop set up (and your mental stability flawless).

Bend over Your Strips for a Grippy Roll

At the point when you're rolling an additional enormous curl, the middle will as a rule, end up breaking liberated from the quilling instrument before you're finished. All you can do by then is to roll the rest by hand. In any case, you can stay away from all that by bending over the strip to begin your curl: the twofold thickness will keep everything where it has a place. To do this, you can either overlay your first strip over, or use two pieces on one another.

Use Nippers to Fix Your Errors

No one's ideal, and regardless of how exactly you are in your work, pretty much every project will undoubtedly have a little blooper someplace. That is where fingernail skin nippers come in. Accessible in any drugstore in the nail care passageway, nippers will let you effectively cut off a lopsided edge or expel undesirable glue after it's dry.

Prepare Your Wipe

A wipe is a quiller's closest companion, and an arrangement is charming. The holder holds your needle-tip stick bottle topsy-turvy so it's all set whenever you need it, while the wet wipe shields your glue from drying out and stopping up the tip. You can likewise use the outside of the wipe to clean any adhesive that gets onto your fingers.

To make your own, simply cut a kitchen wipe and put it inside a little bowl or ramekin. You can even make an arrangement that is sufficiently smaller to fit inside your quilling unit.

Be Companion with Your Eye Pin

So, you left your top off and now your needle tip is stopped up. It's alright, you presumably didn't think about our wipe stunt yet. Be that as it may, there's still expectation! With an eye pin, you can unplug the tip and return to making your specialty. The eye pin's dull end makes it a more secure alternative than a sewing pin. Simply abstain from leaving the eye pin in the tip for quite a while, since the bolt can rust and stain your glued design.

Chapter 6: Cards (Pretty Flowers; Asian Inspiration; Butterflies and Blossoms)

Greeting Cards

Step 1: Normally, for some kind of quilling patterns, you will need to do some sketching, and to do this, you will need a pencil and paper (canvas) if you have one. It's best to sketch on a firm piece of cardboard paper or a paper with a desirable thickness level.

Your sketch could be anything, a house, a flower, a bicycle or car bird, a tree, or anything that comes to your mind.

Step 2: The most fundamental shapes in quilling originate from making circles or curls and squeezing them into wanted shapes.

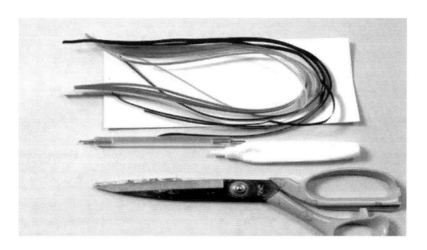

If your ideal blossom sketch needs a leaf-like teardrop shape, simply squeeze one side of the loop, and you will be amazed that you can shape any style by yourself by squeezing, pleating and sticking cycles. Be allowed to explore! Having done the previously mentioned projects above, follow the subsequent stages constantly to finish up.

Step 3: Put a small amount of gum/glue to your shapes at their various points of interfacing with the end edge part of the strip(s) as well as at joinery points. Always prepare your shapes over your sketches and apply a little pressure while waiting for the glue to harden.

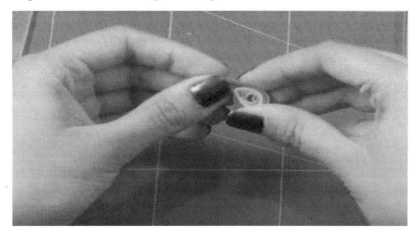

Step 4: From a variety of paper strips, get/pick for yourself one strip and coil the paper around the tip of the quilling tool, which in this case, is the slotted tool.

Step 5: Having done the above, gently pull the coiled strip off the slotted tool.

Then shaped your coil to the exact size you desire and then apply a small drop of glue to the end tail of the paper strip to close you to finish the coiling process.

Step 6: Take any size of colored paper as in your predetermined color and quilting design. Ensure the paper you can use for this background has a considerable gram in thickness.

If you can lay your hands on a desirable colored A4 paper, then you are good to go. But if not, you can also get a paper of any length wideness and cut or trim to any size of your choice, then fold it in half to make the card of hard-back.

Step 7: This part entails the design and decoration of your card. The first type of design to be considered is to try and achieve the rose-like pattern of design by making small cuts on the quilling paper. Then, roll it on the slotted tool and pinching/bending the coil's edges outside to give it that shape of a rose.

You can even join more than one quilling paper to give your card that whimsical and alluring look that everybody might want. Make the same number of coils as you need with various shapes and sizes, utilizing the opened instrument, tweezers device, pleating device, pins, stick, and the whole quilling device is important.

Fix all the objects of different styles and shapes on the front cover and the card's back. Generally, the front of the card keeps more of the quilled shapes and designs. Make your arrangement to be in a specific pattern, or randomly place them depending on the design you intend to make or create.

From experience, it is always better you sketch your predetermined design faintly on your paper cover front for easy object placement, or you could choose to do the sketching on another paper sheet so to serve as a guide.

Don't forget to create a space for some write up. Or you can do your major write-up on the inside of the already-made card. It is either writing directly on it or by attaching a paper-leave on the inside of the card to write on.

Quilled Letters

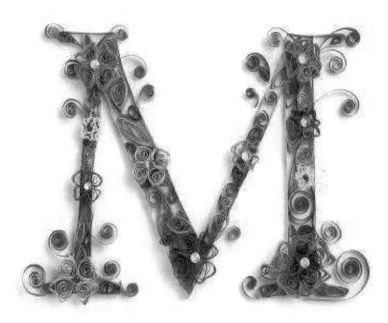

Quilled artworks featuring one letter are one of the most sought-after designs. It is called monogram quilling. When you look at them closely, though, you may get intimidated by the number and intricacy of the straight and curve lines required to form the letters. Don't worry. This project is not that hard to make.

Materials:

- Precut quilling paper or self-made cardstock paper strips of the same width
- Board with white background
- A printed copy of any letter you want to make (the outline of the letter will do)

- Sharp pencil
- Craft glue
- Two tweezers
- Pins
- Scissors or thread snapper
- Cuticle nipper

Steps:

1. Place the printed copy of the letter you want to make on the board.
2. Using your sharp pencil, trace the outline of the letter.
3. Make the different coils you want to add to your artwork.
4. Trace the slightly etched outline of the letter using your preferred paper strip. It will stand out from all of your artwork, so choose a color that looks bright and different from the ones you use for your coils.
5. Fold and curl your paper strip as needed. Attach a paper strip of the same color to cover the entire outline of the letter.
6. Use pins but keep them at least 1 inch apart.
7. Next, glue your paper strip into the board.
8. Leave it to dry. While you wait, plan the coils you will insert in the letter and the coils for its sides and edges. You may also consider adding some wavy lines.
9. Cut the uneven parts of your outline with a cuticle nipper. Get rid of some visible dried glue as well.

Place the bigger coils inside the outline of your letter. Apply glue to the sides and bottom of your coils. You can insert them by hand. Use the tweezers to adjust their placement.

Next, insert the small coils inside. Apply glue to their sides and bottom as well. Use tweezers to put them in.

Add some open coils with tails on the sides of your letter. Glue them properly. Leave it to dry.

Remove the visible dried glue.

Are you satisfied with your artwork? Consider displaying it as wall decor. Has it framed to keep dust at bay?

Try the steps herein to make different letters and numbers as well. You can use your creations as decors for parties.

You may also draw the letters and numbers yourself. You may even draw landscapes, seascapes, silhouettes of people, or outlines of simple items. Find inspiration in your surroundings. You can certainly find one that you can use for your quilling artwork.

Birthday Card

Ribbon: Make two bunny ears and two arrowheads, using full-length grape purple strips. Wrap the center of the ribbon with a 1/8" (3 mm) wide strip.

Lavender Marquise Flower and Flower Buds: Make four flowers for each flower. Roll three marquises, using 1/6 length lavender strips. Make six more marquises for buds.

Lavender Tight Coil Flower Buds: Make four tight coils using 1/8 lavender strips.

Leaves: Make fourteen large and six small leaves. For each leaf, make three-loop vertical husking, using moss green strips. Make four more leaves. For each leaf, make two-loop vertical husking.

Vines: Make six loose scrolls with ¼ length yellow-green strips and two more with 1/6 length yellow-green strips.

Pollen: Make six tight coils, using 1/16 length canary yellow strips.

Heart-Shaped Stem: Fold one (21 cm) long moss green strip in half and curve the ends inward. Glue the ends at the same time to form a heart shape.

Assembly:

1. Glue the heart-shaped stem in the center of the card.
2. Glue the large leaves outside the bottom of the heart-shaped stem and glue the small leaves above them.
3. Glue the lavender marquise flowers outside the heart stem and between the leaves. Glue the vines on the inside of the heart shape.
4. Glue the pollen between the flowers and leaves. Add the ribbon in the center of the heart shape.
5. Add a happy birthday to the center of the card.

Simple Flowers

Another simple flower is a cornflower.

Imagine how delicate it is to get a handmade New Year card with a daisy applied to it! And you can make such a bouquet in an hour.

Instructions:

1. Cut out 8mm-wide and 20cm-long white paper strips.
2. Twist them with a drop.
3. Cut an 8mm-wide and 20 cm-long strip from yellow paper.
4. Make a closed coil.
5. Glue the elements—the chamomile is ready.
6. We should focus separately on creating volumetric colors. For your base, you need a special cardboard cone.

Water lily looks no less original and beautiful on crafts (especially in applications on notebooks). It also needs a cardboard floor.

Instructions:

1. We make 14 drops.
2. Glue 8 blanks onto the edge of the base cone.
3. We glue another five drops to the second stage.
4. The last element is defined in the middle. The water lily is ready.

Simple Heart

Overlay the strip at half, twist one end and then, roll freely by hand until you have made one portion of a heart. Repeat this process on the opposite end, rolling the strip the other way. For this quilling card, you will need:

- Strips of paper
- Cocktail stick
- PVA glue

Butterfly

Art is naturally appealing, and paper quills butterfly is an art. Therefore, paper quills butterfly is appealing to not just the eye, but the mind. However, there seems to be something that ignites a deeper sense of artistic elegance in paper quills butterflies.

If you know how to make paper quills butterfly, you sure would be among the finest artists in the world. Wouldn't you love to be a rewarded fine artist? I see you want to. Now, I will introduce you to the basics and equally expose the secret things that could make your paper quills butterfly unique.

Required Materials for Paper Quills Butterfly:

To arrive at a decent paper quills butterfly, there are a few materials to put in place.

The basic five materials include:

- The quilling paper
- Quilling pins
- Quilling stencil
- Slotted quilling tool

- Dispensing quilling glue

If you do not own any of the tools above, the chances of arriving at something elegant would be quite low. Some persons substitute for other papery materials as a replacement for the traditional quilling paper. But then, the result would either be a distorted finishing or a swaying design.

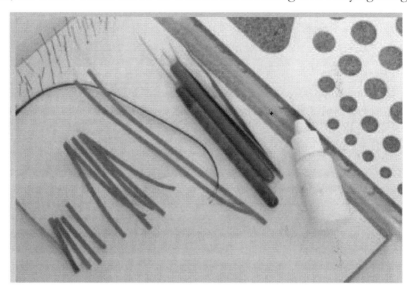

How to Make Paper Quill Butterflies:

Gather the Required Supplies.

For a small butterfly, the required supplies include:

- (4) 1 ½-inch strips
- (6) 3-inch strips
- (2) 6-inch strips
- A 12-inch strip of black slotted quilling tool glue

Optional Tools:

- Needle tool
- Tweezers
- Circle sizing board
- Corkboard and pins

Fold the Strips in the Corkboard:

After you have the mentioned tools in place, punch holes on the corkboard. The hole may not necessarily have to be like what you have in this photo. You may design however way you desire. In this photo, a pink strip is used because it is what I choose. There are more lovely colors, and if you do not mind, I will recommend some colors for you. You may go for something like royal blue, pitch color, or emerald green; if you love pink, no problem.

Arrange the Strips as Shown Here:

At this point, take a studying look at the image above. You can see the looks of the quills. Now, here is how to achieve the design. I believe you have the glue with you because it is needed now. Just as in the picture above, arrange each pink (depending on the color you are using) strip to look the same. Once you have been able to do so, apply the quilling glue, and try not to hold the bottom of the strap tight. Since it may be difficult not to hold it while applying the glue, hold it with less pressure so that each wing is pointy when the glue is dry.

Rose

It is easiest for beginners to sort out schemes with descriptions of the quilling roses, so recommend artisans.

Instructions:

1. Cut out a 20cm-long and 10mm-wide paper strip.

2. Insert the end of the strip into the eye and wrap it three times around the axis.

3. Apply the adhesive with a toothpick and lay the tape at the right angles to you.

4. Make another round with a bell on the needle and drip the glue again.

5. If you repeat steps 3 and 4, place the entire strip. Rose is done.

Chapter 7: Jewelry (Diamond and Double Flower; Silver and Gold Earrings)

Double Flower Finger Ring

Paper quilled flower finger rings are adorable pieces of art. Interestingly; they are easy to make.

1. Join at least 4 quilling paper strips of the same color together to form a long paper strip.
2. Create a 12mm-coil fold from the long paper strip.
3. Make fringes from paper strips using scissors. The paper strip color should be the same unless you wish to use a different color.
4. Curl the fringed strips on the external coil fold and press it firmly to achieve a firmer flower shape—clear varnish by applying a coat to the fringed paper strips and allow to dry.
5. Use craft glue to attach the ornate flower to the ring.

Behold, you have one of the few most beautiful ring arts out there in your palms. Create more until you become a perfect crafter.

Diamond Rose Quilling

Materials Required:

- Quilling paper—any width will work, however, 3/8 inch or 1/4 inch are used most normally. Both are accessible as standard sizes or cut your own strips. Around a 7-inch length makes a decent, full rose
- Quilling instrument—opened device or needle device (I'll use a standard opened equipment for this instructional exercise)
- Scissors
- Paste—I like to use a reasonable gel; likewise, Scotch Glue
- Plastic cover—use as paste palette
- Paper penetrating device, T-pin, or round toothpick—to apply stick

Directions:

1. Cut a segment of 3/8-inch x 7-inches paper.

2. Slip one end of the strip into an opened device from the left. It doesn't make a difference whether you are right or left-handed, as both will have assignments.

3. Hold the instrument vertically in your right hand, the strip in your left, and start to roll the device toward the left. Make a couple of unrests to make sure about the paper and structure the focal point of the rose.

4. Utilize your left hand to twist the strip straight up at a 90-degree point. There's no compelling reason to wrinkle the overlay.

5. Keep rolling the instrument toward the left, turning over the crease as you go. Simultaneously, use your left hand to bit-by-bit carry the strip down to a flat position. I understand this sound ungainly, yet attempt it—you'll before long observe it turns into a smooth collapsing and moving activity.

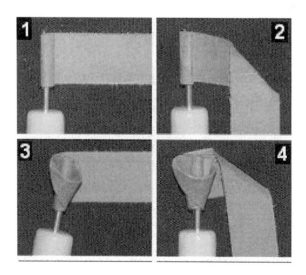

Next, the left hand is bringing down the strip; the right hand is still rolling the device. Now it's an ideal opportunity to overlap and go once more.

Tip: Make another overlap right when you've wrapped up the past one.

The second crease/roll has been finished.

6. Repeat the moving/collapsing the same number of times as it takes to go through the strip—it's just as simple as that.
   Look, a rose is coming to fruition! This is after six or seven folds... notice it's shaping topsy-turvy and would make a decent bud at this stage.

7. At the point when near the end of the strip, detach any overabundance, slip the rose off the device, and allow the folds to unwind. Shape the rose by tenderly turning or untwisting the folds of a piece. Conceal the torn end of the strip by sticking it to the underside of the rose.
   Tip: A torn paper end will be less perceptible when stuck because it mixes superior to a sharp cut. Smooth out the middle crease brought about by the opened device by embeddings and turning the tip of a paper penetrating device or round toothpick.

Quilling Jewelry

Paper quilling jewelry is as old as ages. Today, a large part of the world is practicing the unique art of quilling jewelry, and it's now a trend. From the look of things, diamonds, golds, and silvers may soon lose their relevance to paper-quilled jewelry in the industry. You can make the most exceptional jewelry from paper quilling within some dedicated minutes. It is a matter of paper strips, glue and a few other tools.

Materials Required for Quilling Jewelry:

- Quilling paper strips of varying colors
- Quilling comb
- Slotted quilling tool
- Crimper tool
- Mini mold
- X-acto knife
- Jump ring
- Glue
- Quilling board
- Tweezers
- Plier

Paper Quilled Necklace

a. Create 7 paper strips of varying colors into 7 large petals with more full loops and pinch them into teardrop folds.

b. Fold 2 paper strips of another color into closed coil folds using a slotted quilling tool.

c. Glue the folds to the internal points of 2 outer petals.

d. You need to make the inner petals by creating 5 open coil folds and pinching one end of each to make a teardrop fold.

e. Glue in the inner petals inside the larger leaves.

f. Make a large coil fold and smaller coil folds, as in the picture above.

g. Insert the large coil fold in the middle of the design.

h. Use tweezers to place the smaller coil folds between the sizeable open coil folds and glue them together.

i. Play around with the arrangement of the folds in the larger folds until it's satisfactory. Glue the folds together and allow them to dry.

j. Attach the necklace fastening to make the quilled necklace wearable. You may apply a sealant to keep the jewelry safe from exposure to water.

Silver-and-Gold Teardrop Earring

- **Silver Teardrop Earring:**

It is effortless to make a beautiful silver earring. This guide walks you through making a paper-quilled teardrop earring seamlessly.

1. In this tutorial, I am using just two colors—light and dark silver. Pick your paper strip color according to preference. Moreover, you need 10 paper strips—5 light silver and 5 silver. Make each paper strip into a closed coil fold—more substantial and smaller coil folds.
2. Pinch one end of each coil fold to make a teardrop fold.
3. Wrap another color of the paper strip on each paper strips; repeat the process for all 5 folds.
4. Attach 2 teardrop folds in pairs to form a heart shape. You should have 5 teardrop folds—two heart shapes and one teardrop fold.

5. Glue one heart-shaped fold on the other and place the remaining teardrop fold at the m-shaped part of the glued heart shapes.

6. Create an open coil fold and attach it to the bottom of the pendant. That will be the holder of the jump ring.

7. Attach the jump ring to the single-coil fold alongside your earring.

- **Gold Teardrop Earring:**

It is effortless to make a beautiful gold earring. This guide walks you through making a paper-quilled teardrop earring seamlessly.

1. In this tutorial, I am using just two colors—light and dark gold. Pick your paper strip color according to preference. Moreover, you need 10 paper strips—5 light gold and 5 gold. Make each paper strip into a closed coil fold—more substantial and smaller coil folds.

2. Pinch one end of each coil fold to make a teardrop fold.

3. Wrap another color of the paper strip on each paper strips; repeat the process for all 5 folds.

4. Attach 2 teardrop folds in pairs to form a heart shape. You should have 5 teardrop folds—two heart shapes and one teardrop fold.

5. Glue one heart-shaped fold on the other and place the remaining teardrop fold at the m-shaped part of the glued heart shapes.

6. Create an open coil fold and attach it to the bottom of the pendant. That will be the holder of the jump ring.

7. Attach the jump ring to the single-coil fold alongside your earring.

Chapter 8: Ornaments (Easter; Halloween and Christmas)

Paper Quilled Snowflake

It costs a few minutes to make and hold snow in your palm. That sounds great, considering that you would love to play around with snow even in summer! The children and adults love to warble in snow. The elders may not be virile enough to jump around snow, which is why hand-crafted snow folds are preferable.

Interestingly, you require no much vigor or energy to build snow. Yes, you read that right, and you'll learn just how possible and easy it can be.

Paper quills bring our imaginations to reality, and one of such is the cold snow. Instead of packing and feeling the roof with cold snow, make quills snowflake a companion. This section quills pattern brings the snow close enough that you may not miss natural snow any longer.

I know you would love to learn this art, and I am willing to show you how it is done. Do you fear this design would be the most difficult of all you have seen so far? Trust me; your mind is playing games because the snowflake paper quills are as easy as any other easy-to-do paper quill.

With projects like this, you will learn to become a better quill artist rather than sit all day and be praising the quill creativity from others. It is time to get the praises too, and I trust you to do even better than what you find here.

Within a few minutes, these simple instructions will reconcile your curiosity and further make you a unique paper quill artist.

Materials Required for Paper Quilled Snowflake:

- A pair of scissors
- Quilling paper strips (blue and white)
- Pencil
- Quilling glue
- Glue dispenser
- Quilling pins
- Geometric compass
- Quilling tool
- Ruler
- A plain paper sheet

Quilled Snowflake Folds:

Here are the number of folds and types of folds needed with regards to the snowflake quilling done in this guide.

Materials:

- 18 blue quarter-length tight coils
- 6 white length tight coils (54cm)
- 6 white length marquis (54cm)
- 6 blue length teardrops (54cm)
- 6 blue half-length tight coils
- 6 white quarter-length marquis
- 1 white half-length tight coils

How to Make Paper Quilled Snowflake Ornaments:

1. Paper length/width: 54cm x 5mm

Pick a length that best suits the occasion. In this project, we are using 5mm-wide and 54cm-long paper strips. Depending on your requirement, you may opt for something different. However, for this task's purpose, use a paper strip of 5mm-wide and 54cm-long to follow up better. Use a ruler to measure the length for perfection, carefully.

2. Create a circle on the white paper

Insert the pencil and carefully stretch the compass about 5cm to 6cm-wide. Place the compass at the center of the white sheet and carefully rule a perfect circle. Finally, use the pencil to divide the circle into six visible equal parts.

3. Drawing the floral

It may be difficult for a beginner to draw the floral. For now, make exactly the design you find here unless you are an expert willing to do something different. To come up with the snowflake design, you may visit online guides on how to draw a snowflake because several models could be used to develop the project. If you are okay with what is on this photo, then follow suit. You can achieve the decorative effect by doing the following:

- Draw a half-cm circle at the center of the larger circle.
- Draw 6 small circles around the small circle.
- As in the picture above, draw 6 more oval-like shapes.
- Make another 6 longer oval-like shapes round the 6 small circles.
- At the tip of the shorter oval-like shapes, create a large and a small circle as in the picture.
- Create four more circles at the tip of the 6 longer oval-like shapes, as in the picture.

4. Crafting the various folds

In this project, I am using three different paper folds including marquis, coil, and teardrop folds.

Crafting the marquis folds: The marquis fold is an eye-shaped fold that involves pressurizing both ends of the folded quilling paper for the marquis effect.

Fold all 6 of the 54cm-long white marquis around the quilling tool or any available tool. Withdraw the quilling tool and pad each of the 6 folds gently with your fingers.

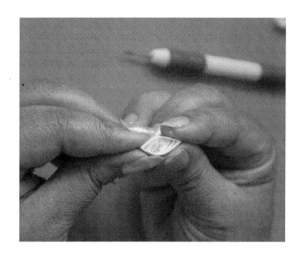

Press both ends of each white 54cm folds gently until you achieve an eye-shape. Release the pressure for the fold to loosen, pick and apply glue to the edge of the fold.

Crafting the coil folds:

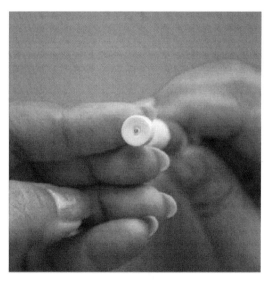

Wrap a 54cm fold around the quilling tool.

Retrieve the quilling tool and glue the flapping edge of the fold.

Crafting the teardrop folds:

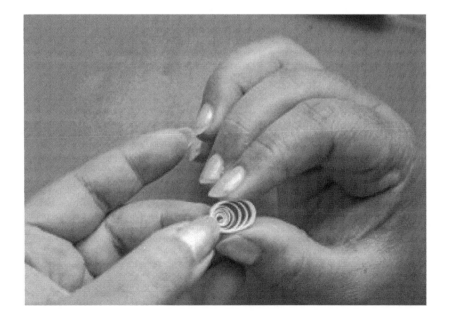

Wrap a new fold around the quilling tool. Retrieve the quilling tool and release the fold to loosen.

Firmly hold one end of the fold to create a tip-like design as in the picture and apply it to the flapping edge.

5. Applying folds to the drawing

Try to place the marquis, teardrop, and coil folds in the corresponding areas of the circle. Make sure they each match the diagram, or it may distort the design.

Place each fold on the corresponding shape on the circle. Begin with the central coil fold, followed by the surrounding circular coil folds.

Place all 6 marquis folds, followed by all 6 teardrop folds in their corresponding positions. Repeat the process for the coil folds by placing a coil fold on each of the teardrop folds.

Place the remaining coil folds on the corresponding positions surrounding the teardrop and marquis folds. Place the half-done snowflake paper quill on a flat surface and apply glue to each fold carefully. Allow the glue to dry, and your lovely snowflake is ready.

You may optionally coat with a sealant to protect against water. Send your paper quills to loved ones as winter or summer gifts. During winter, make as many snowflake quills as possible and decorate your surrounding with them.

Guess what? Your crafted snowflake paper quilling can stay for as long as you desire; so far, you handle with care and coat with sealant.

Peacock Design

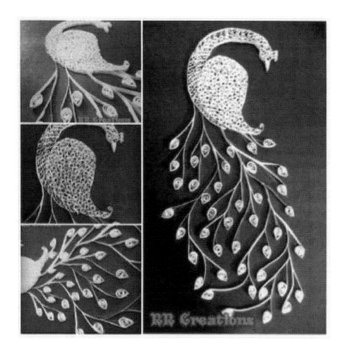

Structuring a peacock follows a similar methodology of drawing and plotting. It relies upon the quilling strip used and the mix. In the event that you need to get the specific design on the spread picture of this book, then you need to consolidate different strips to accomplish a similar outcome.

Since this is a novice's guide, we will use a single shading strip. At the point when you become sure of your aptitudes, you would then be able to continue making delightful shading mixes.

Materials Required for Peacock Design:

- Quilling strips (5mm—cream or white-hued)
- Black thick paper
- Craft paste
- Scissors
- White shading pencil
- Quilling device

When you have all these, you are prepared to begin this stunning project.

Step 1: Getting started.

Next is to draw the unpleasant blueprint of the peacock's body close by its quills. This would give you a harsh thought of what number of quilled parchments would be required and would likewise help in making staying more straightforward.

When you are finished with the necessary number you'd like, create them and checkout if it fits. Whenever happy with the result you have, feel free to stick them solidly.

Step 2: Making the neck of peacock

For the neck, I used the beehive technique of paper quilling. This may take a bit of time and requires tolerance. Cautiously organize and stick the quilled strips to each line in turn.

Step 3: Outlining

When you've finished the body and neck of the peacock, and the stick strip has dried, apply the paste and run a sort of piece along the outskirt to give a shape to the work as outlined previously.

Step 4: Connecting the Feathers

Measure the lines between each quill independently, slice and take advantage of the plume—associating every in a steady progression.

This is entirely troublesome—however, with caution and persistence, you'd accomplish it.

Step 5: It's done!!!!

You can use this as a casing to enhance your divider or as a gift to somebody exceptional.

Isn't it lovely?

Paper Quilled Christmas Wreath Ornament

The Christmas tree can't find its splendor on a Christmas without the famous green wreath. When the tree lights up, especially during a cold night, the tree beguiles the sight of every human, and the wreath stands out so uniquely.

Again, it will be splendorous to adorn the Christmas tree with the wreath.

The paper quilling art is an elite class of art on its own. Most interestingly, we can bring the green wreath to life with a couple of paper strips, glue and a quilling tool. This guide discloses the beginner basics of adequately creating a DIY wreath ornament.

It's quite an easy art to create; let's find out how.

Materials Required for Paper Quilled Christmas Wreath:

- Paper strips—light green, dark green, and red colors.
- Craft glue
- Slotted quilling tool

How to Make the Paper Quilled Christmas Wreath:

Step 1: Make dark green closed coils:

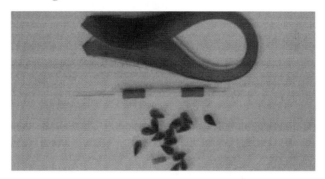

Curl the dark green strips around the slotted quilling tool to a closed coil fold. Pinch one end of the fold to make a teardrop fold (petal-like shape).

Note: About 15 teardrop folds would be enough for a mini Christmas wreath.

Step 2: Arrange the dark green teardrop folds:

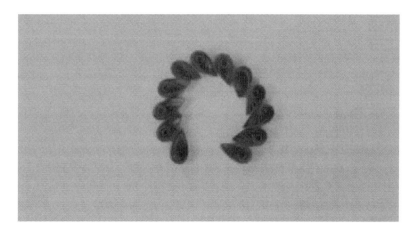

Arrange the teardrop folds in a circle as in the picture above and glue the folds together to make a rounded wreath.

Step 3: Add the red and light green teardrop folds

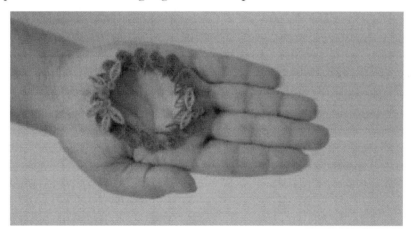

Just like the dark green teardrop fold, design the red and light green teardrop folds. Make the red folds and light green folds come in small and large sizes. Glue some read teardrop folds at the top and down part of the wreath.

You now have a great wreath! Take photos of the wreath and share it across social media platforms. You may as well use the garland to decorate your office desk, send as a card to loved ones or place it in a visible place for its charming beauty.

Christmas Time

The Christmas season is always here, and alongside it comes the yearly race to convey and part with occasion cards to your loved ones. Regarding Christmas cards, a few of us like to go with the old reserve box sets (JAM offers a few exquisite choices) while others like to take the custom-made course. If you are more inclined to place yourself into the latter classification, this post is for you.

The individuals who stay up with the latest with paper-making patterns are presumably acquainted with quilling. For the individuals who are not, here is a short clarification. Quilling is the act of twisting and molding portions of the paper to make bigger ornamental shapes and plans. Here, I will tell you the best way to use quilling to make your own delightful and brightening Christmas wreath cards!

You Will Need:

- One standard quilling instrument (A sewing needle will likewise work.)
- Bright hue red paper
- Dark red paper
- White paper or cardstock
- Scissors
- One hot glue gun (with glue)

Instructions:

Step 1: Cut slim, 11-inch-long portions of green paper. These strips should be generally even in width. However, they shouldn't be exact.

Step 2:

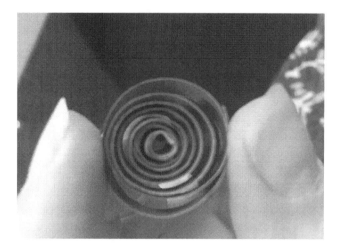

Utilizing your quilling device or needle, fold the initial segment of paper into a winding. After it is completely moved, eliminate it from the device and let it mostly disentangle. It should resemble this.

Paste the remaining detail of the twisting set up with your paste firearm. Repeat this progression until you have enough green twisting's to frame a full wreath.

Step 3: Pick a sheet of paper or card stock to use as the body of your card. For sturdiness, card stock is suggested. Before sticking it set up, lay put your green twisting's on your card surface as you might want to show up in your completed item.

After your design has been decided, use your glue gun to glue your wreath together on the card's surface!

Step 4: Since your fundamental wreath shape is finished, you can proceed onward to making the bow. To start the bow, cut a few red and dim red paper pieces, as you did with the green paper in step 1. After these strips have been cut, pick two similar tone segments to make them into quilled tear shapes. These will turn into the inward most bits of the bow.

Step 5: To make a teardrop shape, wind your segment of paper around the quilling instrument or needle, similar to what you did to make basic circles. While eliminating the paper from the device, just allow it to disentangle part way instead of releasing it. How much you allow it to disentangle will influence the size of your tear shape.

After this winding has completely loosened, hold the central point of this twisting with the forefinger and thumb of your non-dominant hand while pulling tenderly outward. Use your dominant hand to pull the external bit of the twisting the other way while squeezing to shape a point (the head of the tear). Paste the remaining detail of the shape set up with your glue gun.

Step 6: After you have made two teardrop shapes of a similar tone, take two pieces of other shapes of red and firmly fold them over these shapes. Paste the remaining details set up. Next, take two portions of the main shade of red you used and freely fold them over the external surface of the shapes you just wrapped. Squeeze the head of everyone, so it coordinates the states of the focal points. To complete the two parts of the bow's head, do this again with the contrary shade of red. Shown below is the teardrop shape you began contrasted with a finished portion of a bow.

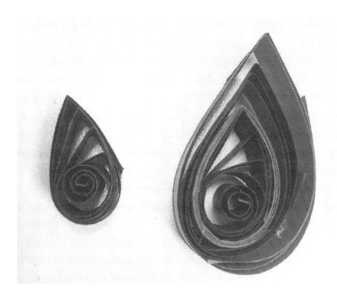

Step 7: Make center for your bow by winding a tight, little hover of red paper and wrapping a piece of the other red shade around it. Paste this round shape along with your glue gun, and afterward, stick all lace pieces onto the wreath in any size you want!

After these are in place, loosely curl a few more red strips of paper and glue them in place to create the bottom/excess bowstrings.

Your wreath card is now complete! If you wish, you may use writing utensils to include a message such as "Merry Christmas," "Happy Holidays," or "Hi, Mom" within the wreath!

We hope that this craft helped to brighten up your season. Happy Holidays for all of us!

Christmas Tree

Supplies Needed:

- Green craft paper
- Quilling strips in different colors
- Quilling tool
- Pencil or pen
- Scissors
- Glue or glue stick

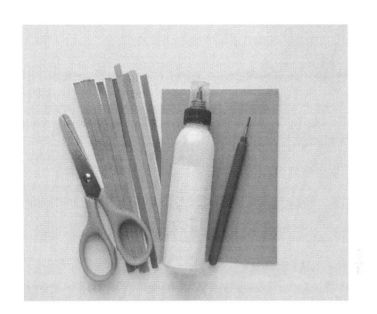

Instructions for Making the Paper Quilling Christmas Tree Ornament:

1. Take 6-inches-long green quilling strip and use the opened quilling instrument to loop the whole strip into a tight curl.

2. Separate the coiled strip from the tool and allow it to loosen up a little. Prepare a total of 15 similar loose coils.

3. Use 3.5-inches red strips to make little tear shapes.

4. Now, make a couple of loops utilizing quilling strips in arranged tones. You can make them free or tight—whatever you like. Make four earthy colored free loops too.

5. Take a rectangular bit of green specialty paper and accumulate all the green free loops arranged in steps 1 and 2. Use the paste to stick 5 free curls in an orderly fashion towards the lower side of the green-hued make paper.

6. Keep staying lines of the free green curls, one over the other. As you move upward, continue lessening the number of curls in a line by 1, so you end up with a triangle design.

7. Stick the red tear shapes on the top end of the triangle. Paste them along with the pointy end out, so you get a 5-point star design.

8. Cut the art paper along the Christmas tree's external edge, including the red star.

9. Use the various brilliant loops to embellish the tree by essentially sticking them on either side. Include four earthy colored curls on the tree's base side in a square example to make the tree trunk.

10. At long last, include a little globule as the focal point of the star design if you like. Allow it to dry, and it's finished!

This quilling Christmas tree ornament is very multipurpose. You can join a string and balance it on the tree with a similarly adorable paper quilled wreath ornament. However, you can likewise make a handcrafted Christmas card with it. Or then again, why not connect it to a piece of card to cause it to go with these Christmas gift tags? It couldn't be any more obvious; a little exertion and a couple of strips sure go far!

Snowman

Christmas crafts are popular and good gifts. Right now, I will tell you how to create a Christmas paper quilling snowman.

There are many quilling paper Christmas ornaments on Panda hall. Most of them are cute and uncomplicated to make. The materials are quilling papers in different colors and some pearl beads. You need no other professional skills in making this DIY snowman craft.

Supplies Needed:

- 3mm pearl beads
- Quilling paper(bright red, green, yellow, black, white)
- Model
- Scissor
- Tweezers
- White glue
- Rolling pen

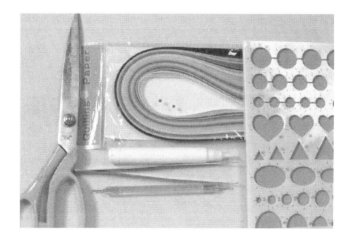

Step 1: Make a few paper quilling roundabout globules

Take around 4 pieces of white quilling papers, fold them into enormous round dabs, and stick the end solidly. Take around 2 pieces of white quilling papers, fold them into a round globule. Make the other 5 white roundabout dabs and other 2 red round dots, and 2 green roundabout dots with a similar length. Stick all the little roundabout globules around the large round dab as shown in the picture.

Step 2: Include another roundabout example and pearl dots

Roll a white roundabout dot with around 3 pieces of quilling papers; stick 2 pieces of 3mm blue pearl dabs on it as eyes. Cut an off bit of yellow quilling paper, move it to a round globule, make sure the internal part is higher than the external part.

Step 3: Make an oval bead

Fold a dark quilling paper into a roundabout globule, placed it into the 10cm opening and stick the end, and squeeze the roundabout dot into an oval dab.

Stage 4: Make the final Christmas snowman plan

Stick the dark oval dot to the top of the snowman as a cap; at that point, roll other dark round dots as shown in the picture. Cut off red quilling paper and dark quilling paper, move them a few circles and loosen them to make them look as in the image. Stick the end of the red quilling paper with the dark quilling paper together. Stick the end to the left round globules of the snowman, and stick 3 blue pearl dots on the enormous roundabout dab, as in the picture.

Here is the last look of the Christmas paper quilling snowman:

Do you love this bright and charming paper-quilling snowman? I completed this DIY snowman in 15minutes. You can likewise find it out how to make a Christmas snowman at home. It fits for another person to begin his/her quilling paper DIY project. Now, my instructional exercise on the most proficient method to make a Christmas snowman has concluded. Have a pleasant attempt!

Christmas Lights

Is it safe to say that you are searching for a novel subject to do with your children? It would even be an extraordinary subject to do with kids for a winter or Christmas celebration. With only a couple of devices, they can make this remarkable arrangement of lights to show for these special seasons!

List of Supplies:

1. Craft paper, white
2. Quilling strips
3. Slotted paper quilling tools
4. Scissors
5. Craft glue or glue stick

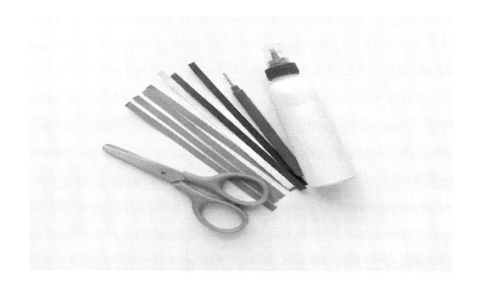

Instructions to make the craft:

Step 1: Take 20 inches hued quilling strip, and use the opened quilling device to curl the whole strip.

Step 2: Once the coiling is finished, take out the tool's coiled strip and let it out.

Step 3: Hold any one side of the release coil to form a teardrop shape and paste the open end to secure the shape.

Step 4: Take 3-inches-long white shaded quilling strip and make a free loop shape with it.

Step 5: Press 2 inverse sides of the free curl to frame a focal point shape.

Step 6: Get the tear shape arranged in the last advances.

Step 7: Supplement the focal point shape made in step5 into the tear shape, through the hole of any loops close to the bent end; the bulb design is prepared. Also, make more bulb designs.

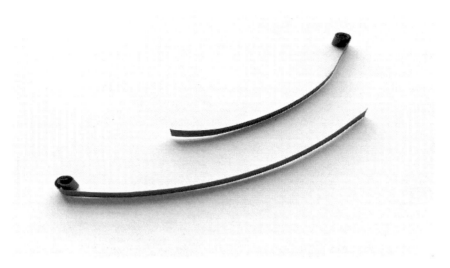

Step 8: Now, take 6-inches-long dark quilling strip and make a little whirl on any of its ends. Use around 2 or 3 cm to make the whirl design.

Step 9: Cut out a white specialty paper or cardstock paper for the foundation, or you can pick any shading you need.

Step 10: Paste the two dark whirled strips on the paper by making a slight breathtaking example with them. Paste the two strips in 2 lines, keeping, always, 1-inch hole between them.

Step 11: Take a bulb example and paste it on the paper by keeping the bent end contiguous with the dark strip (the bulbs' fundamental wire).

Step 12: Individually include the remainder of the bulbs to fill the dark strip.

Allow the glue to dry, and have fun!

Chapter 9: Home

Paper Quilled Teardrop Vase

Your vase is beautiful, but you can enhance the beauty by making it into something alluring with paper quilling art. It is quite simple, and a matter of quilling folds into teardrops using at least four different colors if you desire a gradient effect.

This guide discloses a simplistic way of fashioning a vase with the paper-quilling art. In a matter of minutes, your first ever-alluring quilled teardrop vase should be ready.

Required Materials:

- Paper Strips

In this guide, I am using a small set of paper strips with gradient colors. You may use one color, but you won't achieve the gradient effect.

- Vase

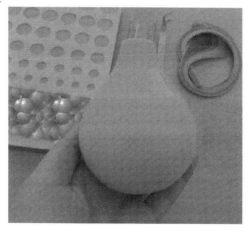

The vase must not be too curvy. It will be challenging to place the teardrop folds on an overly curvy jar. Get something smooth, and that would support the placement of folds.

- Paper glue

The glue must be such that it can glue the quilled paper on ceramic.

- Quilling needle

A cocktail stick wouldn't be a bad idea, but a quilling needle is ideal.

- Quilling board

The quilling board comes in various sizes. Depending on the size you would prefer, get a quilling board for the paper quill. Alternatively, you may use create circles on a plain sheet and use it to determine the sizes of each of the folds you make.

- Slotted quilling tool

Necessary to make folds. You can alternatively use a chewing stick.

How to Make Paper Quilled Teardrop Vase:

1. Create Coil Folds

Pick and place each quilling paper on the quilling tool. Try to make the placement at the tip of the quilling tool to be able to control the spiral shape.

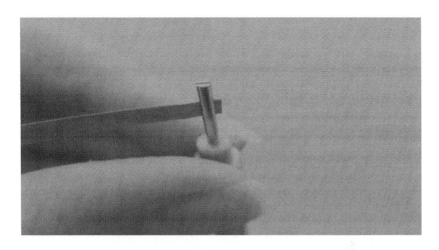

Fold each coil around the quilling tool carefully.

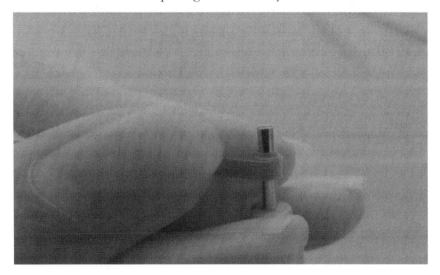

When done, hold the paper firmly but not too tight to give it excellent shape.

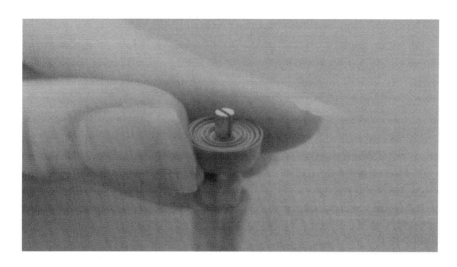

Withdraw the coil folds from the quilling tool and place them carefully in the quilling board and allow for loosening. In the absence of a quilling board, make sure that each fold fits the size of the circle you created on a plain sheet.

Repeat this process for all the quilling papers.

2. Make the teardrop effect

Withdraw each of the coil folds from the quilling board.

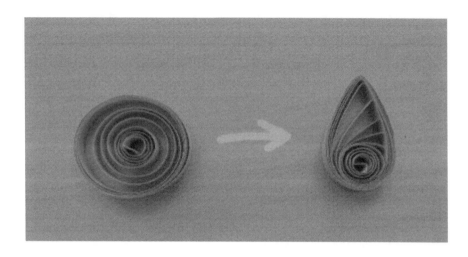

Place your two fingers at one end of the coil fold.

Gently, press that end to form a tip.

Hold it tight with added pressure.

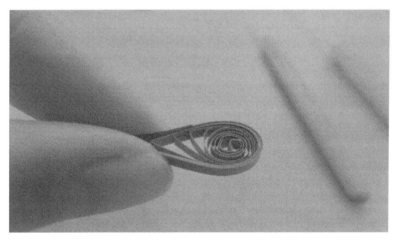

You should now have a well-made teardrop fold.

Place the teardrop fold on the quilling board and repeat the process for every paper.

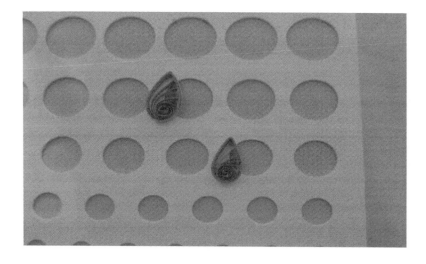

3. Decorate the Vase with the Teardrop Folds

Pick up, clean your vase, and arrange the teardrop folds according to their colors.

Beginning from the bottom of the vase, apply paper glue to the teardrop folds and glue each fold to the jar.

Continue the gluing process and fill up the bottom of the vase. A darker fold color is preferable if you're beginning from the bottom of the vessel.

Repeat the gluing process for the second row of the vase. This time, the color of the fold should be lighter than the color of the fold at the bottom for the gradient effect.

Again, attach each teardrop fold to the vase in the third row. Try to use a color different from that of the second row, as in the picture above.

Finally, use a lighter color for the fourth row to complete the gradient effect.

You now have a lovely quilled teardrop vase.

Note: Depending on the size of your vase, you may attach teardrop folds for more than four rows. If you intend to cover the entire vessel with the teardrop drops, endeavor to resize the teardrop folds when you reach the curvy part of the vessel. Retaining the longer teardrops will result in a distorted quilling in that area.

Now that you have an elegantly-crafted quilled teardrop vase, you may send it across to loved ones or share your knowledge with friends.

Paper Quilled Flower Frame

Materials Required:

- Quilling tool (any of your choice)
- Paper quilling strip (we'll be using different colors, feel free to use any color of your choice, here I used blue, purple, white, yellow)
- Glue
- Paper swab or toothpick (for applying the glue)
- Pearls

Directions:

1. Make as many teardrops as you can, some bigger than some (three different sizes of teardrops, the bigger ones should be more with different colors).
2. Equally, make lots of marquis shape and closed coils.
3. Now attached the pointed ends of the bigger teardrops in groups of six using the glue, do the same for the other marquis, matching the same colors together. Make enough flowers to go around your frame completely.
4. Now attach the pearl to the mid-point of each created flower.
5. Place this around your frame and glue it in place.
6. Next, fill up the spaces between using the marquis and glue them in place.
7. Next, use the closed coil to fill up the even smaller spaces left and also glue it in place. Voila, your frame is ready. You can place a greeting card in the middle, or even place the picture of a loved one there.

3D Flowers

It's time to step up your game a little as beginners as we'll be designing a 3-D flower from scratch.

Materials Required:

    a. Paper strips (different colors)

    b. Quilling tool

    c. Tweezers

    d. Glue

Directions:

1. Create lots of marquis and further convert most of it into a slug.

2. Now attach these in groups of three (same colors), place the elongated marquis at the middle and the slugs at the sides, use the glue and hold until its dried, repeat these for all the

created marquis and slugs, now wrap each group of 3 with a different color of the paper strip.

3. You should have 17 petals in total.

4. Arrange them in groups of 5 attaching the pointed ends with the glue.

5. Now make 3 large closed coils with variations of colored paper strips as illustrated, make it as large as you like.

6. Apply glue to one side of each closed coils and place it in the middle of the arranged group of 5 flower petals.

7. To have the desired 3-D effect, place the flower on your palm and press the middle with the attached closed coil inward.

8. Using glue, attach different shades of paper strips to form a stronger bond of the paper strip, use as many colored strips as you want.

9. When it is thick enough, use a tweezer to coil the ends of the modified paper strip. This forms the tendrils.

10. Make two shorter versions of this without coiling.

11. Place two uncoiled short tendrils at 90° to each other, facing upward. Then place the coiled tendril in the middle.

12. Next, use the glue to attach 3 slugs to one of the uncoiled tendrils, place the 2 green petals at the top of the other uncoiled tendril and finally place the last slug at the point where the curve starts beside the coiled tendril.

13. Now place your prepared flowers at the bottom of the tendrils arranging them as illustrated. And that's it, your 3-D flower is ready.

Chapter 10: Gifts

Quilled Butterfly Pendant

1. Make paper strips of different colors into teardrop folds. As in the picture above, make the folds into big and smaller sizes.
2. Arrange the teardrop folds into a butterfly shape as in the picture above, glue them together and allow them to dry.
3. Coat the quilled pendant and allow it to dry.
4. Finally, fit in the jumping ring, and attach to a necklace.

Paper Quilling Dolls

Materials:

- Color papers (paper weights 130-180grams)
- 3mm (1/8") and 6.5mm (1/4") color paper strips (paper weights 130-180grams)
- Different lengths and thicknesses of the strip may require more or less strips to make the same circle size. I used the 21.5 x 27.9cm (8.5 x 11") cardstock papers which weigh 176grams to cut pieces.
- This type of paper strip maybe tricky to find. You can use a knife or trimmer to cut the paper into strips. I think the most convenient and fastest way is to use shredders (size 6.5mm (1/4") and 3mm (1/8") strip-cut).
- Poster paper (use for making the base, or you can use other paper instead).

Tools:

- Slotted quilling tool
- White glue
- Scissors
- Ruler
- Utility knife
- Cutting mat

Optional tools:

- Circle sizer ruler
- Mini mold
- Size 6.5mm (1/4") and 3mm

- (1/8") strip-cut shredder
- Paper trimmer
- Bow punch and hole punch
- Tweezers
- Paintbrush
- Bamboo sticks

- **1.1 Making the Base:**

(A tight circle)

Prepare a white poster paper 55.8cm x 71.1cm (22" x 28"). Cut the white poster paper into 6.5mm x 55.8cm strips.

A paper shredder provides a convenient and fast way to make quilling strips. If you don't have a shredder, you can use a utility knife or other cutting tools to cut.

Using a thicker and longer poster paper can save time when rolling the circles.

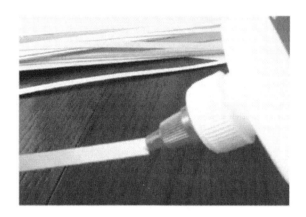

1. Apply a tiny amount of glue at the end of the strips.
   If you accidentally put too much on, you can use a toothpick or brush to apply evenly.

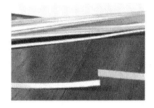 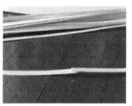 

2. Glue 9 strips end to end to make a long strip.

3. Turn it in a way that makes you feel comfortable. You can place your thumb and index finger on both sides of the paper strip to keep it neat.

4. Maintain tension on the paper strip while you are rolling. When the piece is fully gone, gently pull the tool off. Don't let it expand. Pull it tight.

5. Apply a small amount of glue on the end. Hold it for a few seconds until the glue is dried. Now, we have a tight circle with a diameter of 4.2cm.

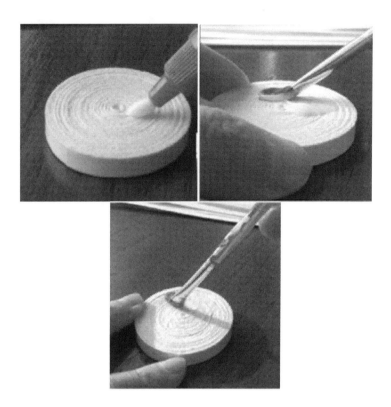

6. Squeeze the glue on the circle, and use a brush to apply it evenly. Wait for it to dry, then the base is done.

- **1.2 Making Basic Head Shape:**

To make a head, you need 3mm (1/8") wide skin-colored strips. You can use a mini shredder or another cutting tool to cut skin-colored paper.

1. Glue 13 strips end to end to make a long strip (Different lengths and thicknesses of the strip will need different numbers of pieces to make the same circle size). Make two long strips.

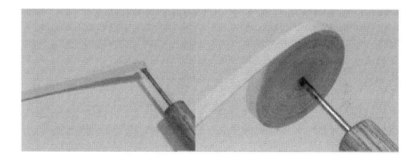

2. Use the tool to roll the long strip to make a tight circle with a diameter of 3.2cm.

After, pulling the circle tight, glue the end and hold it for a few seconds until the glue dries.

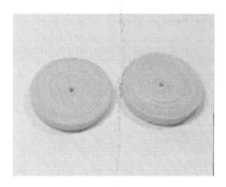

One head requires 2 tight circles.

3. Use your fingers or mini mold to push gently on the tight circle, shaping it into a dome as shown. Make 2 of them.

4. To make sure the domes do not collapse, coat them with a layer of glue on the inside. Let it dry.

5. Apply glue around the edge of each dome. Place the 2 dome edges together and press closed. Make sure it is even all the way around. Let it dry.

6. Apply glue all the way around the joint, then take a strip of paper and glue it all around. When you have gone around once cut the remaining piece and glue the end. Your basic head shape is now finished.

- **1.3 Making a Student Doll:**

Materials:

- 3mm (1/8") wide skin-colored paper strips (28)
- 3mm (1/8") wide blue-colored paper strips (5)
- 6.5mm (1/4") wide light blue-colored paper strips (10)
- 6.5mm (1/4") wide blue-colored paper strips (7)
- 6.5mm (1/4") wide brown-colored paper strips (3)
- 6.5mm (1/4") wide green-colored paper strips (8)
- 2.5cm wide green-colored paper strips (2)
- 2.5cm wide creamy-colored paper strip (1)
- 2.8cm wide orange-colored paper strip (1/2)
- 1 base
- 2 small eyes (use the 2mm hole punch or use scissors.)

Making the Student's Doll Head:

1. Make a basic head shape using the 28 pieces of 3mm (1/8") wide skin-colored paper strips (Please see and follow the instruction in 1.2 Making Basic Head Shape).

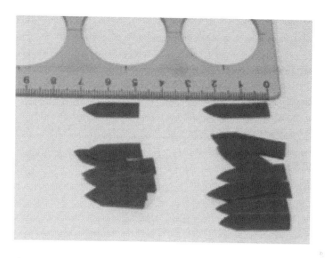

2. Cut the three 6.5mm wide brown colored strips into 2.5cm-long and 2cm-long pieces.

3. Use the hole left from the quilling tool to be a nose. Stick a 2.5cm-long strip on the lower part of the head and then stick another one overlapping the first one slightly. Repeat all the steps till you finish the semicircle.

4. Stick the 2cm-long strips on the face to become bangs. Leave the points free of glue.

5. Use the remaining strips to stick on the upper part of the head as shown. Leave the points without glue.

6. Stick the strips on top of the head as shown, leaving the points without glue. Use the fingers to fold up the ends to make them feel like upturned hair.

Making the Student's Doll Body:

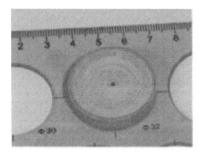

1. Glue ten 6.5mm-wide strips of light blue and three 6.5mm-wide pieces of blue end to end to make a long strip. Use the long piece to make a tight circle with a diameter of 3.2cm.

   Note: When making a circle or cylinder, always glue the end.
2. Use fingers gently pushing up the quilled paper into the ruler as shown in the picture.

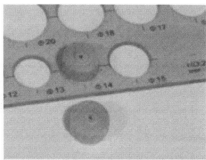

3. Use two 6.5mm-wide strips of a circle and create a cone shape around blue to make a tight circle with a height of 4 cm. Concave the point with a diameter of 1.4cm. Make 2 of the cones slightly to help stick them to the head.

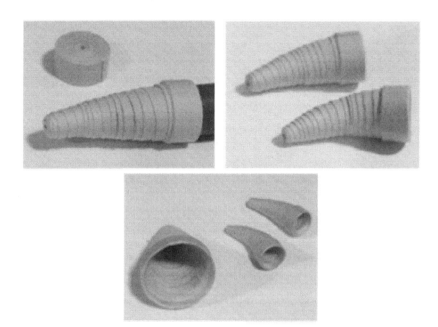

4. Use a pen gently pushing out the circles and create cone shapes around 3.5cm-tall as shown. Then slightly Coat the inside of the bend the sleeves. Body and envelopes with glue. Let dry.

Assembling the Body and Making a Student's Book:

1. Glue the head, body and sleeves together. Let dry.

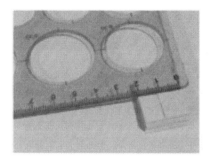 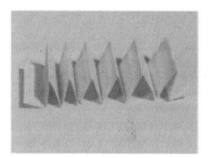

2. Fold the 2.5cm-wide milky-colored strip back and forth in 2cm increments as shown. This will be the pages.

3. Fold the 2.8cm-wide orange-colored strip around the pages as shown. Make sure the two ends come together evenly. Cut off the excess.

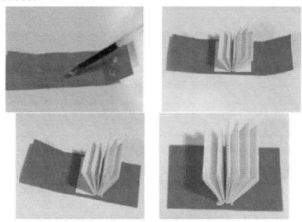

4. Glue the pages and cover together as shown.

Making the Hood:

1. Glue four 3mm-wide strips of blue end to end to make gently flatten the cone.

2. Use this strip to make a tight circle with a diameter of 2cm gently push up the ring and create a collapse. Coat the cone shape, as shown, inside with glue.

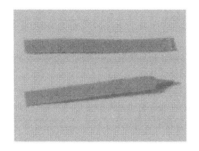
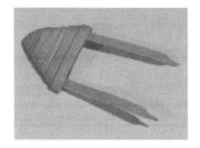

3. Use a 3mm-wide blue-colored strip to cut two 3cm-long pieces. Pinch one end, and glue the other end into the hood.

4. Glue the book at the front of the body and the hood at the back as shown. Let dry.

Making the Student Doll's Legs:

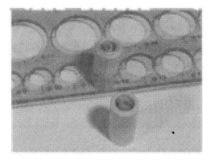

1. Roll the two 2.5cm-wide green-colored strips into two cylinders with a diameter of 1.2cm as shown.

185

2. Apply a tiny amount of glue at the end of a 6.5mm-wide green-colored strip. Attach it to the end of the cylinder and wrap it around making an outer ring. Pull up the circle as shown and coat the inside with glue.

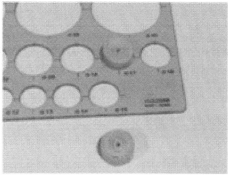

3. Glue three 6.5mm-wide green-colored strips together and make it into a tight circle with a diameter of 1.7cm. Make 2.

4. Glue the cylinders on the circles. Let dry. Now two legs are complete.

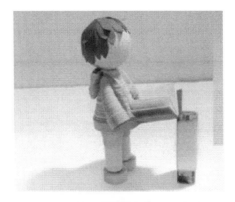

5. Glue the legs to the body (Support until dry).

Making the Student Doll's Hands:

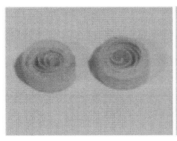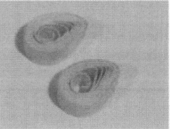

1. Roll a 3mm-wide skin-colored strip into a loose circle with a diameter of 1.2cm and glue the end. Pinch one side of the ring to make a teardrop. Make 2 of them. Glue them into the sleeves as hands.

2. Finally, glue the eyes to the face and stick the doll on the base. Now your student quilling doll is completed.

Chapter 11: Other Paper Quilling Projects

Paper Crafts-Quilled Butterfly Headband

Materials Required:

- Shaded cardstock (one sheet every one of dim purple, light purple, white, and pink)
- Toothpicks
- Paste
- Mod
- Quilling device
- Scissors
- Gemstones in pink and purple
- Sparkle

- Plastic paste
- Headband

I printed out a thought of my motivation a delightful pink and purple butterfly. Also, gathered together my devices. For this undertaking, I used a little quilling device. You can discover them at most art stores. I trust I paid only a couple of dollars for this device and I've used it for a considerable period of time! Likewise, I like to use Aleene's Tacky Glue on the grounds that merely like it says in the name, it is cheap. I can work considerably more rapidly as the paste works quickly and dries clear.

I can work considerably more rapidly as the paste works quickly and dries clear.

I used my little paper shaper to cut around 5 every (1/8") segment of each shading. On the off chance that you don't possess a paper shaper, you can surely do this with scissors.

Start by sliding the finish of a pink strip into the space of the quilling device. At that point, bend the instrument and start winding the paper strip around the end of the device.

Curve the device and wind the paper until the whole strip is twisted around the end of the instrument. Handle the edges of the paper and slide the device out. You currently have a decent winding.

Squeeze one finish of the winding to make a tear shape and include a spot of crude paste to the furthest limit of the paper strip. You now have one tear drop formed winding.

Make one more tear formed winding in pink, and afterward 2 spirals that are squeezed at each end. Paste each pair together as appeared. Take

190

some of the light purples and include dabs of paste along its length. Use that light purple strip to fold over a lot of pink spirals. Repeat with the next set.

Utilize a similar strategy to make four dull purple spirals. Paste them together. Enclose the upper pink wings with dim purple strips like you did the light purple.

Include light purple strips around the dim purple wings, and afterward include white pieces around every one of the four sides. Now, slice a toothpick to the length that you might want the body to be.

Stick along some of the dim purples and wind it around the toothpick, absolutely covering it. Paste the wings to one another and to the sides of the toothpick as appeared. Cut two 1/16" extensive portions of dim purple for the receiving wires, and loop the end with your quilling device. Paste-on.

Spot the butterfly on plastic (so it won't stick) and coat it with Mod Podge for security. When dry, flip it over and cover the opposite side. Allow it to dry completely. Include a couple of stick gems for shimmer. At that point, include specks of paste along the edges of the wings and sprinkle sparkle to finish the look. Tap off the additional sparkle and allow to dry

And there you have it. A lovely shimmering butterflies! You can do loads of things with this little paper animal. You can enhance a casing with it, cause a cooler magnet, to make divider craftsmanship, or do as I do and make a headband out of it.

Quilled Flower Locket

Materials Required:

- Quilling paper—dark, (1/8-inch standard width strips) or slice your own light to medium weight paper utilizing an art blade, metal-edged ruler, and cutting mat
- Quilling instrument—opened device or needle device or substitute a hardened wire or even a biscuit analyzer
- Scissors
- Ruler
- Tweezers
- Paper penetrating device or mixed drink stick—to apply stick
- T-pin or glass head pin—to shape blossom focus
- Non-stick surface—use as paste palette and work board. An acrylic sheet, waxed paper, or Styrofoam plate are fine as well; I for the most part use a container top
- Clammy material—clingy stick fingers and quilling don't blend
- Gems pincers—2, mine are level nose

- Bounce ring—silver
- Memento—silver (the one I used is from Michaels; read progressively about it in Part 1)
- Strip—3/8-inch width; around 24 inches

Directions:

1. Make the blossom: roll a 3-inch dark tight loop on quilling instrument of decision. (You'll discover more data about picking a device in Part 1) Glue end set up before slipping curl off the device. Tip: if the strip has a torn period, the paper will follow easily when stuck, making the loop look overall quite round.

   Shape the loop top by squeezing a T-pin or a glass head pin against one side to make an adjusted vault.

   At that point apply a modest quantity of paste inside the arch to save the bend.

2. Make 10 matching ring windings by wrapping a length of quilling paper multiple times around a dowel. Test with various dowels to figure out which one creates the right curl size for the pendant you are using. Most likely one of your device handles will work; I used a paper piercer.

   Slide loop off the dowel, fix it if necessary by pulling the strip end, and squeezing one spot to make a tear shape. You'll feel embarrassingly clumsy from the start with the wrapping/sliding/squeezing, yet after a little practice, it turns out to be natural.

   Paste end and trim overabundance paper.

3. On a non-stick work board, stick tips of tear petals around the domed focus taking consideration to space them equally.

4. Whenever the paste has gotten an opportunity to set for a few minutes, apply a slender covering of glue to the rear of the bloom with a fingertip or mixed drink stick. Use tweezers to fixate the flower on the memento. It's ideal not to squirm it into position as this will leave a snail trail of paste. Allow the blossom to dry for the time being... make an effort not to be impatient.

5. The following day, turn open a bounce ring with forceps and slip it through the fixed memento ring.

   Close hop ring and string onto the strip. Polish off with a customizable sliding bunch so the neckband can be slipped here and there over the head.

The memento is prepared to wear or provide for somebody on your vacation list; maybe a little youngster who may be roused to have a go at quilling as well. Children for the most part love to plume!

Chapter 12: How to Preserve Your Paper Quilling Projects

I know what it takes to complete a single project and no new or advanced crafter can afford to let the plan get ruined. However, this preservative method is split into two sections so we can attend to 2D and 3D designs separately. But in the end, you should be able to choose the technique you feel you are okay with.

Preservative Methods for 2D Quilled Projects

- **Plastic Sheet**

This is one of the most natural techniques to preserve your quilled paper project. It has an opening made with OHP transparent sheet and frame that accommodates your craft.

With this, you are sure your coils are fully protected from dust and getting pressed with a heavy landing. Simply check any stationary shop around your neighborhood to get these OHP sheets.

- **Varnish Spray**

Though this might be a little bit expensive compared to the first method, it keeps your projects clean and polished. It enables the quilling paper to become stiff and dries fast but be mindful of the one you get because a bad one will alter the color of your designs. Ensure you spray at a distance of at least 15cm.You can get this in any of your craft and hobbies store near you.

Preservative Methods for 3D Quilled Projects

- **White Glue Coating**

Fevicol is a good sample of white glue to look at because it's readily available in most stationery stores and you can easily apply this directly with a brush.

Though you can also use it for 2D projects, ensure it is smooth evenly when applying. To make it smooth, mix with a 2:1 portion of Favicol and water to make the smooth application consistent.

If the water is too much, the coil will loosen and make your project look awkward. While, if the mixture is also ticked, you are likely to damage it.

This method will make your 3D project looks elegant and improves the color of the strips. Carryout the coating more than once in 15-20 minutes to strengthen the project. Note, this sealant will act as dustproof but not water repellent. You can also find some other brands that are water-resistant and lighter in a texture that suits both 2D and 3D.

- **Nail Polish**

This method is quite cheap and readily available at cosmetic stores. Nail polish provides an intense sheen and at the same time hardens the strips.

This is best for 3D and closed coils but don't use this for projects that are likely to be exposed to heat, sun, or water because it can melt, peel off, or even develop cracks.

Nail polish is water-resistant but not waterproof.

Now you can go on with your favorite design and pattern with the hope of using any of the above methods to keep your project alive.

Chapter 13: Striking Paper Quilling Artists

Striking and legitimate people are available in each field of life and the specialty of paper crafting itself. To give you more inspiration when making paper quilling projects, recorded underneath are the famous and legitimate world-class paper quillers, their profiles, remarks and aides for apprentices in the authority of paper quilling.

Yulia Brodskaya

The Russian craftsman is well known for her tastefulness and itemized work of art. Albeit, by and by situated in the UK, she says "typography is my second love after paper and I'm extremely upbeat that I've discovered a method of joining the two. Having said that, I would prefer not to prohibit non-grammatical mistake-based structures, I'd prefer to deal with various activities."

The research paper realistic is known to be what Yulia depicts her works, as accuracy and outright enumerating are fairly unmistakable components of them. Yulia began as an artist and visual craftsman, however changed to paper artistry after her first paper project. She expected to structure a unique presentation for her name on a handout and used paper quilling. The rest is history.

Farah Al Fardh

Farah, the Emirati craftsman is alluded to as a pioneer in the Arabic world as respects to paperwork. She is obviously the first Emirati craftsman to be respected with the privileged "Endorsement of

Accreditation" from The Paper Quilling Guild in the UK, as she visits to stun the world with her astonishing works, her fantastic enthusiasm for unusual 3D paper quilling models. I am very sure you will pay a visit to her helpful and fascinating YouTube channel.

Ashley Chiang

Yulia Brodskaya could be supposed to be the motivation to have birthed this paper quilling sensation. As indicated by Ashley here and there in December 2012, she went over Yulia's work and was shocked by the art and quickly picked incredible enthusiasm for quilling practice. Within a year, she was displaying at the stand-out show in Chicago, and from that point forward her development in paper quilling has been upward and onward as it were. Her works are interesting for sharp and splendid hues just as eye-catching structures which make her work fulfilling to take a look at. The American resident has demonstrated to be an extraordinary sensation in this field.

Ann Martin

Ann Martin is a creator and paper craftsmanship fan that works in "custom quilled marriage authentications, ketubot, and wedding greeting mats that are reasonable for confining, just as paper gems." She has a site that centers around paper quilling and different kinds of paper expressions. I especially like the site in light of the fact that Ann includes top-notch paper expressions and artisans, and is a phenomenal wellspring of data if you need to stay aware of current patterns in the realm of paper creating.

Sena Runa

The Turkish craftsman is known to be a wayfarer of new domains in artistry, as she makes for herself her particular style, which in her words gives her an opportunity. Different to most artists, she makes her own strips accordingly to her signature of all her pieces of work. She's additionally nitty-gritty with hues as she manages home designs of all sort. Every single one of Sena's structures happens to be merry as she unmistakably fuses the ink into her paper delineations. She is recorded to have sold around 180 works throughout the whole world. She owns a site which I suggest you visit and will discover fascinating and charming works.

Jitesh Patel

The Europe-based craftsman is perceived for his production of ongoing prospects that guides paper-quilling customers to get by in their unquenchable universe of structures. He is gifted and skilled in heading and delineation and unlike some other craftsmen, has thought that it was helpful to all to manufacture a library containing components for unique plans. His structures are supposed to be comprised of lines in their most straightforward structure, anyway, they are so fragile.

Bavani Ratnam

In her words "quilosophy is tied in with sharing the specialty of paper quilling" the paper quilling master who has practically been in the field since the mid-21st century is known for the production of enriching expression cards and many others. The Malaysian magnificence is said to have higher interests and dreams albeit still in the quilosophical field, she works a ton with paper, however, she's unmistakably not restricted to it.

Dr. Jiji

The Indian dental specialist holds a record for her work which entered the general records for her 101 works of paper quilling which was displayed at a presentation in Thrissur in some occasions in the first half of 2016. She started her plume project in 2012 and self-prepared in every last bit of her leisure activities, including painting, but paper quilling remains her preferred activity.

Ideally, through these little extracts of such incredible works, you'll find the motivation to plunge into the profundities of this hypnotizing paper work, and find your own exceptional paper quilling styles come to you. As intriguing as these specialists seem to be, we are sure the universe of paper quilling has a lot more.

Conclusion

Paper Quilling is extraordinarily simple. It is easy to complete. You don't need to put in a lot of your time and effort to get familiar with the exchange by any means. You should simply acquaint the fundamental aptitudes and procedures of the trade and there you have it! With a little practice and repetition, you will before long become a specialist.

The different devices and materials that are essential for this exchange are commonly less expensive to drop by. They are likewise locally accessible. You don't need to invest a lot of your energy and effort to source them from a remote place off.

On the off chance that you are continually stressed out, this craftsmanship is an extraordinary way of getting away from the distressing circumstances. Throughout working the paper strips, you get the opportunity to scatter pressure and the development of anguish. This prompts a loose and made height.

Finally, the exchange additionally adds to the incitement of the mind. This is because of the way that it improves the progression of blood in the body. Thusly, you get the opportunity to remain fresh, alert and fit as a fiddle. You may wish to give it a shot while concentrating to support your concentration and consideration.

You may well have noticed that the specialty of quilling is an incredible endeavor without a doubt. The various potential advantages it brings along are beyond any reasonable amount to disregard or treat with less reality.

This is the reason you are, by all methods, encouraged to consider checking it out on the off chance that you have never. All the best as you begin in the field of paper quilling!

One of the most significant characteristics about paper quilling is that it is fun and simple to make. When you've aced it, structuring any sorts of quilling works will be your preferred leisure activity.

There are different fascinating artworks that you can make out of quilling paper, it just takes, knowing the fundamentals, strategies, and ideas to frame designs of your choice.

The most ideal approach to begin, in the event that you are a beginner, is to discover motivation, you need to contemplate quilled craftsmanship that you want, and use it as a springboard for making your own breathtaking structures, maybe, soon enough you will be astounded how individuals will appreciate your work and use it as a motivation for their quilling projects.

Individuals who make a wide range of art using quilling paper began as a fledgling, testing and playing with various types of shapes and procedures to make simple, but viable specialty designs. When you have your blueprint, the inventive opportunity is all yours.

It's just about paper crafting that includes slender segments of paper into one-of-a-kind 3D shapes. These little paper structures can be used to finish various types of things you may be shocked about. Actually, you can make quilling designs that are complementary.

I explicitly composed this book to help you with creating abilities and methods that will cause you to make your own show-halting structures when you have learned paper quilling, which is the craft of folding and molding pieces of paper into improving plans. I can guarantee you that you will start to deliver beautiful quilled works while building your aptitudes.

This book is supplied with supportive tips and it also has adequate fundamental information to paper quilling that will empower you to practice this art without stress. It additionally gives tips for the best devices and sorts of paper to use for your quilling projects. Particularly, as a novice and the basic shape to begin with the goal for you to ace paper quilling and turn into a pro in under seven days.

It won't just instruct all of you to think about paper quilling, it will likewise hand over to you a mainstream expertise that can make a salary for you when you make your most-loved pastime and become imaginative with the artwork.

It would be ideal if you read and give me a survey of how you feel about the book. You may wish to focus on supporting your attention and thought.

Glossary

3-Dimensional Figures—an influential character or an article or shape that has three measurements—length, width and tallness

Anniversary Card—a card given to recall the date on which an occasion occurred in an earlier year.

Butterfly—a nectar-taking of creepy-crawly with two sets of enormous, normally splendidly shaded wings that are secured with minuscule scopes. Butterflies are recognized from moths by having clubbed or expanded receiving wires, holding their arms erect when very still, and being dynamic by day.

Christmas Wreath—a: a brightening course of action of foliage or blossoms on a roundabout base a Christmas wreath. b: a band of interweaved flowers or leaves worn as a characteristic of respect or triumph: festoon a tree wreath.

Coil—Loops a length of something wound or organized in a winding or arrangement of rings.

Crimper—otherwise called wire crimper, creasing instrument or pleating forceps, is a device used for creasing connectors onto wires.

Diamond—a precious stone, one side of which is level, and the other cut into twenty-four triangular sides in two territories which structure an arched face pointed at the top

Double Flower—depicts assortments of blossoms with additional petals, frequently containing blooms inside blossoms.

Gold-Plated—secured or featured with gold or something of brilliant shading. Having a satisfying or flashy appearance that hides something of minimal worth.

Happy Birthday Card—it's a welcome card given or sent to an individual to commend their birthday.

Learner—a newcomer or amateur, particularly an individual not used to the difficulties of pioneer life.

Locket—a little decorative case, regularly made of gold or silver, worn around an individual's neck on a chain and used to hold things of nostalgic worth, for example, a photo or lock of hair.

Marquis— (in some European nations) an aristocrat positioning over a tally and under a duke.

Necklace—a fancy chain or series of dots, gems, or connections worn around the neck.

Open Markets—an unhindered market with free access by and rivalry of purchasers and vendors.

Opened Circle Sizer—it's a disentangled adaptation of our circle format board with gap estimates that arranges with the entirety of our quilling packs.

Paper—material produced in dainty sheets from the mash of wood or different stringy substances, used for composing, drawing, or imprinting on, or as wrapping material.

Paper Quilling—is a work of art that includes the utilization of portions of paper that are rolled, molded, and stuck together to make enlivening plans.

Pastime—an action done consistently in one's relaxation time for joy.

Peacock—a male peafowl, which has long tail quills that have eye-like markings and can be raised and fanned out in the show.

Pre-Cut Strips—cut into size or shape before being showcased, gathered, or used: precut filet of fish; precut development materials.

Preserve—look after (something) in its unique or existing state.

Quilling Brush—looks precisely like an afro brush with metal prongs. It is used for making paper curls and paper blossoms that are prevalently used in paper quilling artistry structures and scrapbook plans.

Quilling Needle—it's one of the most generally used quilling devices. It permits you to make little focuses on rolls and parchments which creates increasingly appealing quilling.

Rolling—moving by turning again and again on a hub.

Semi-Circle—some of a hover or of its circuit.

Shredder—a machine or other gadget for destroying something, particularly archives.

Slug—an extremely cleaned earthly mollusk that ordinarily does not have a shell and secretes a film of bodily fluid for security. It very well may be a genuine plant bug.

Snowflakes—a chip of day off, a padded ice precious stone, commonly showing fragile six-fold balance.

Square Shape—a plane figure with four straight sides and four right points, particularly one with inconsistent nearby sides, as opposed to a square.

Strips—a plane figure with four equivalent straight sides and four right points.

Structure—an arrangement or attracting delivered to show the look and capacity or activities of a structure, article of clothing, or another item before it is manufactured or made.

Tear—molded like a solitary tear.

Tear—pull or tear (something) separated or to pieces with power.

Triangle—a plane figure with three straight sides and three points.

Trick—keep from developing or growing appropriately

Tulip—a bulbous spring-blooming plant of the lily family, with strikingly shaded cup-formed blossoms.

Tweezers—a little instrument that is made of two thin bits of metal which are joined toward one side and that is used to hold, move, or pull exceptionally little articles.

Valentine's Day Card—a card communicating adoration or love, sent, frequently secretly, to your darling or satirically to a companion, on Saint Valentine's Day.

Youngsters—pincers, pliers, forceps, or a comparative device for holding or cutting.

Quilling Patterns For Beginners

A Complete Guide To Quickly Learn Paper Quilling Techniques with Illustrated Pattern Designs to Create All Your Project Ideas

by Brenda Sanders

Table of Contents

Introduction

Paper quilling is the art of rolling, shaping, gluing and embellishing strips of paper. This method is also called paper filigree or merely quilling. You need a tool called a quill to produce the standard coiled shape of the paper. You then glue the paper at the top and shape the coils to form numerous designs, such as flowers, leaves and other various decorative designs.

This ornamental technique of using paper goes back to the Renaissance, when nuns used the coiled paper designs to decorate book covers, bookmarks and spiritual items. At this time the most frequently used type of paper was the gilded edges of the pages of books. The nuns coiled the little strips of these gilded edges to imitate the iron latticework of the period. It was an art practiced by mostly women in the 18th century and was one of the techniques that young girls needed to discover as part of their studies. The colonists brought the art with them when they emigrated to America. The majority of the quilled paper designs that have actually been secured are of spiritual artwork.

The art of quilling did die out for a time, but has just recently become a very popular craft. This is because of the low cost of the paper materials needed to make designs to embellish boxes and invitations and especially pages of scrapbooks, with the increased interest in scrapbooking.

The tools you need to get going in quilling are very fundamental, such as; strips of paper, something to wind the strips around and glue. The strips of paper can be cut in widths of 1/8 inch to I inch, but the majority of people use 1/8 inch strips. You can select the paper in whatever weight you desire, however the standard is construction paper, which can be found in a range of colors. The winding tool can be a toothpick or a needle, but you can likewise check out a craft shop to buy a specifically created quill.

Other tools that you require include sharp scissors for cutting the paper and a ruler to make sure that you cut all the strips the very same size. You can cover a piece of corrugated cardboard with wax paper, instead of using the top of a table. This will keep the glue from getting onto the table. You need to also have a moist fabric at hand for cleaning the glue off your fingers.

A few of the simple designs you can start out with include:

- A V-shape style includes folding the strip of paper in half and rolling the ends of the outside of the paper around the quill. You have to roll the paper far from the inner crease.

- Feelers include rolling just part of the strip of paper. You can get this design by folding the strip in half or by using an in-folded strip.

- Coiling the paper either loosely or very securely around the quill can give a peacock eye.

Using quilling varies from decorating photos that can be framed and hung, to celebration cards, from picture frames to 3 dimensional objects. Flower designs are often a favorite for a lot of quillers, but animals, scenes, landscapes and balanced patterns are all highly effective. The very nature of the art of quilling gives it a more three dimensional designs and adds new possibilities to pictures.

There are many ways for coiling your paper; French and Italian nuns used to use goose quills for this reason. You can use a needle or a toothpick, however it is better to buy a specially developed slotted quilling tool, these are relatively affordable and very effective. You can use any kind of white glue as long as it dries clear.

The great feature of the art of quilling is that it appropriates for all levels of capability. You can rapidly discover how to make easy styles and fundamental shapes, but more advanced quillers can make highly intricate, ornate and delicate designs. Some quillers specialize in three dimensional designs.

Imagine sitting at your kitchen table. In front of you are some narrow strips of colored paper; a tool that looks like a hat pin, and a little bottle of craft glue.

Paper quilling is a craft that invites newbies with open arms. All it takes is to learn every fundamental strategy, from rolling various shapes to scrolling, fringing, looping, and weaving paper.

Soon, you'll be displaying your custom-made quillwork with pride, making unique quilled gifts for family and friends, and sharing new methods and concepts with other paper filigree crafters.

Chapter 1: Basics Of Quilling Paper

Quilling can be an enjoyable art and it can be an excellent way to enliven your scrapbooks, customize your gifts, and make your handmade cards remarkable and special. Quilling undoubtedly is an easy method to reveal your creativity. For sure you would love quilling if you like paper crafting and making designs on your own.

Quilling has long been used in cardmaking. Now we know the paper is wound around a piece of quill to produce the basic coil. These coils are used to form various ornaments and patterns that are similar to pattern work.

The Renaissance period had seen French and Italian nuns and monks who are using quilling in decorating cards, covers of books and religious items. During those times, they use paper strips that were trimmed from edges of books. These strips were rolled in order to produce the quill shapes.

During the 18th century, this particular technique in cardmaking became popular among the groups of elite ladies. It was included in the list of one of the things that they can do without getting tired, physically or mentally.

Further, the Americas had also seen quilling spread across the continent, and used not only in cardmaking but in other forms as well. Many artworks can be seen on stands, cabinets, cribbage boards, purses, picture frames, baskets and wine coasters. Quilled lockboxes are also popular on storage boxes with drawers. There are times that this technique is used together with other design methods such as embroidery or printing.

Today, quilling had already started making a comeback. Obviously, it had gone through a lot of changes and transformations as it passes from one generation to another. New styles, materials and techniques are continuously being introduced and this caused a lot of expansion opportunities in the cardmaking industry.

Since more and more people are getting into the art of quilling, more and more types of paper are being produced to give options for quillers. Some paper types are: acid-free quilling paper, graduated quilling papers and two tone quilling papers.

The acid-free quilling paper is a great choice when doing cards or scrapbooks. It is guaranteed to last long without affecting the other elements of your design such as pictures. On the other hand, graduated quilling papers are an exceptional choice for decorations. It has solid colors on the edges, then gradually fades to white. Or it can also have light color as a base then gradually fades to solid or darker color towards the inside. Lastly, the two-tone quilling paper functions very similar to the graduated one, but this one has the same color and varies only in intensity.

Its comeback and increasing popularity in many parts of the world continue to promote the art to people from all cultures, of different ages and walks of life. What used to be an exclusive activity for the elite has become a pleasurable art exercise open for everyone to do.

Paper Type

Quilling paper is available on the consumer market in over 250 colors and measurements. It can be divided into numerous categories, like solid-colored, two-tone, acid-free, and other assorted parcels of quilling paper. It is readily available in various measurements, such as 1/8", 1/4" and 3/8" or 3mm, 5mm, 7mm, and 10mm paper parcels. 5mm is the most widely used size.

Acid-Free

As the name plainly suggests this is a is completely acid-free paper. The quality makes it an outstanding choice for making scrapbooks, rubber stamping, and creating frames for images. It guarantees your project to last a lifetime, without any adverse effects on the framed image or album.

Graduated

This kind of paper offers an exceptional want to decorative quilling tasks. The edges have a solid color that gradually fades to white. When using a Graduated paper, a quilling ring begins with a dark shade and faded to a lighter side. On the contrary, some graduated papers begin as white, or a lighter shade, and they later gradually fades into a solid, darker color.

Two-Tone

The appearance consists of a concrete color on one side and a relatively lighter color on the other side. With two-tone paper the color stays the same, however, the strength of the color is different. The main use of this quilling paper is to give a desired level of softness to the quilled subject. It has the capability to quill numerous papers in a single spiral.

The Tools You Will Need

To start with, you should have the materials needed. The essential materials you need in quilling are the quilling paper strips, curling tool and a clear glue. The paper strips are usually lightweight card stock cut into different strips. The standard and most frequently used size is 1/8" but you can have narrower strips like 1/16" or much broader strips such as 1/2" to one inch. The size of the paper strips would depend largely on the design you want. If you desire a style with finer details, the narrower strips would be best. Paper strips are likewise in different colors to improve your designs.

Aside from these 3 materials, you might also need tweezers, a corkboard to work on, pins and toothpicks to help you apply glue to your designs.

Making The Designs

To start, it would be of big help if you have a pattern to base your work on. This will be your guide to quilling your first style. Be patient, as quickly as you have to master the different techniques in making the basic coils, you can have your own time to discover more special designs.

The basic thing to note in paper quilling is to make coils using your curling tool. Depending on the pattern you have, you can make tight coils or lose ones, and you can also make those specialized shapes like the teardrops, the square, the marquis or the eye shape, you can learn them one by one with techniques like pinching the sides of the coiled paper strips to make the shape. The teardrop shape, for instance, which is a typical shape that makes up most quilling designs is made by making a loose coil with your curling tool and pinching one side of it using your thumb and your forefinger to produce a corner on one side, and make it look like a teardrop for a raindrop.

Basically, your style will utilize fundamental shapes like the loose and tight coil. From there, you can make a different idea of shapes consisting of the spirals and scrolls. You can likewise find ideas on styles and patterns from the internet or from others that will help a lot as your guide to quilling your first art piece.

Mounting Your Design

Dealing with a corkboard can be a fantastic idea to help you pin your design before lastly gluing them on your card or paper. You can make use of a toothpick and tweezers to help put the glue on your finished design and help you install great coils. A clear and fast-drying glue is preferred by many to have a clean finish. As soon as you will be dealing with your own, you will ultimately know the difference and discover your own choice with your materials and tools.

As soon as you mastered this basic guide to quilling, you can then move on to more specialized tasks.

What length of time does Paper Quilling take?

Once you learn the fundamental shapes, it does not take long to make beautiful quilled creations. You can spend hours on larger and more detailed styles if you like. Large quilled patterns are typically masterpieces that stand alone and can be framed for show. Most of the designs you'll most likely make when you are quilling will be smaller products to embellish other crafts you are doing so feel confident that it does not need to take the whole day just to make a few quilled flowers; although your good friends might think so! The terrific aspect of quilling is that it looks a lot more difficult than it really is to do!

Quilling paper is a great way of having fun and a beautiful way to be imaginative with the standard coils and scrolls you'll discover how to make. You'll be happily surprised with the works of art you can produce with just a couple of different kinds of quilled pieces. Simply remember that you need to have a little bit of persistence (especially as a novice quiller) because you are working with little tools and small notepads. Each small coil or scroll will be simply one small part of the total design.

Remember to have fun and make your designs as comprehensive and intricate as you'd like. Take time for some trial and error as you learn and you'll quickly be impressed at how rapidly you can make some really cool quilled styles.

Advanced quillers might spend hours and days or even weeks to produce a really involved style. Some are even 3 dimensional which is actually neat however of course takes a fair bit more time to be elaborate and so comprehensive.

Chapter 2: Materials and Tools
Required For Paper Quilling

Quilling is such a versatile art that you can use it anywhere. You can make quilled greeting cards, photo frames, name tags, invitations, scrapbooks. You can also use shapes made by quilling to decorate a box or a flower vase. Or simply you can take a beautiful sheet, make a quilling pattern on it and get it framed to be hanged. The list of its uses is endless. The creativity is yours. You can also make 3D models by quilling as the coiled paper is strong enough and does not get squashed.

Quilling Paper Strips

These come in an untold variety of colours and also in different widths. The most commonly used width is 1/8inch however you can also purchase strips that measure 1/4inch, 1/2inch and 3/4inch. These are used mainly for making fringed flowers or creating 3D pieces.

You can cut the paper strips yourself however, they must be cut with great accuracy otherwise the coils will not look as good. For this reason it is probably more practical to buy paper already cut for you.

Needle Tools and Slotted Quilling Tools

These should be the first tools you get and you may find, depending on the patterns you want to make, that you can stick with just these two for quite a while.

Scissors

You will also find out that you need scissors in a minimalist kit in order to cut your paper strips to the right size or even make your own strips.

Circle Template Board

Since the circle or coil is the basic shape for most patterns, a circle template board can be another useful early addition to any quillers' toolkit as it enables you to accurately measure the sizes of different circles and therefore make more precise designs.

Tweezers

Tweezers are useful for handling your different quilling shapes, especially coils, when working carefully and creating more intricate designs.

A Curling Tool

You can use several different items to curl the strips of paper into coils. Some people use hat pins, toothpicks, a slotted quilling tool or a needle quilling tool. If you use the pins or needle type tools you will have to start the coil by rolling the paper around the center of the tool. When you are a beginner this can actually be quite difficult to perfect so purchasing a slotted quilling tool is probably a good idea. The paper is gripped in the slot making it easier to roll and keep the tension right to produce the correct size of coil. The only slight disadvantage is that the slotted quilling tool had a tendency to leave a little bend at the end of the paper in the middle of the coil.

Glue

Everyone has their preference of which type of glue they prefer to use. The only advice I can give is in the beginning to choose a good quality craft glue that is white and tacky in substance. Be sure that it turns clear when dry. Craft glue is another essential that you need in order to start as it will hold your coils together and is also essential in creating other shapes. If you are starting with a minimalist toolkit then craft glue and a needle tool or slotted tool are your most basic items.

Once you become accustomed to making paper coils you can use any sort of item to curl the paper - many seasoned quillers do finger rolling too!

Quilling Crafts Board

This is not really an essential item but one which will make life a little easier. This board gives you molds of numerous sizes which you can drop your coils into so that they can open up to a uniform size.

Quilling Fringer

Again possibly a non essential however if you wish to create say fringed flowers this tool will allow you to cut the quilling paper quickly and easily.

Fringing tools are ideal for creating beautiful flowers as they make small fringes/cuts in your strips of paper which are often used to make different types of flowers.

Quilling Comb

Once you become more ambitious and you are ready to learn a different quilling crafts technique this tool can help you make zig zag shapes and cascading loops.

Chapter 3: List Of Things That Can Be Made From The Craft Of Paper Quilling

Quilled flowers are really popular because they are so gorgeously made with paper quilling, you will quickly discover that there are so numerous more patterns that you can quill besides simply flowers. Just about anything you can consider, you can quill! From animals to lettering to cars and trucks, you can quill all sorts of patterns using the standard quilling shapes (coils and scrolls) you have found out how to make. The possibilities are actually unlimited considering that you have complete control over the way you develop a style with the fundamental quilling shapes. Quilling is an art type so similar to any other art, you can make anything you'd like and have your ended up piece of artwork appearance unique.

Quilling designs can be used to jazz up any scrapbook or card, even for kids, because you can quill all kinds of toys, automobiles, animals, and other products that bit boys enjoy to decorate the pages of their scrapbook. Just like scrapbooks can have a variety of styles, so can your quilled creations. You can make quilled lettering or style concepts for each page of your scrapbook or homemade card no matter what style, season, or holiday you are celebrating. Try to make all types of different patterns and images when you find out the basics of coiling paper and you will quickly discover that your creativity will cut loose method beyond paper flowers. You'll certainly want to try making a variety of animals, trees, cars and trucks, Christmas designs, and so far more.

Pretty soon people will be appreciating your work and using it as inspiration for their quilling projects.

1. Paper Quilled Monogram

Experiment and have fun with different shapes and techniques to develop this simple but effective monogram. The innovative freedom is all yours as soon as you have your outline.

2. Autumn Tree Greeting Card

Celebrate the autumn season by sending your buddies welcoming cards embellished with a lovely quilled fall tree. Even if you have never made a quilled craft before, you will have the ability to create this card in no time. It is simply made from eye-shaped quilled coils to represent the leaves and fundamental coiled strips to make the trunk of the tree. The simpleness of the design radiates elegance, and the best part is the tree is so easy to make.

3. Quilled Snowflakes

It's never ever early to begin thinking about Christmas crafting. Collect the kids and make these beautiful quilled snowflakes to decorate your Christmas tree. They are so lovely, you can even use them as affordable gifts for individuals on your Christmas list. Nearly everyone will treasure a gift that you made with your hands, it makes the present that far more special.

4. Quilled Ombre Colored Teardrop Vase

This stylish quilled teardrop vase is a terrific task for starting quillers. Simply glue teardrop shapes in gradients of color onto a vase. This job can be made in under an hour. Who doesn't enjoy a craft job that's quick and easy, however still looks so upscale?

5. Quilled Paper Posies in a Basket

This quilled basket of flowers has a sweet vintage appeal. Frame it for a charming new piece of wall art to await your house or to give away as a gift.

6. Contemporary Quilled Angel

Kids, and adults too, can make this modern quilled angel in less than 15 minutes. Can you think of an entire Christmas tree adorned with these angels from top to bottom? Because they are so easy to make, it's certainly possible. You can rapidly craft enough for your entire "Angel Tree" in a number of hours.

7. Green and Gold Quilled Teardrop Earrings

Make some earrings on your own or for a present. Paper Zen shows how to add a golden metal shimmer to your quilled earrings to give them an extra little bit of enjoyment.

8. Quilled Flowers Decorating a Cake

The next time you need to make a cake for a unique event, decorate it with crepe paper kumquat branches sprinkled with the cutest quilled daisies.

9. Quilled Flower Pendant

Paper quilling naturally offers itself to jewelry tasks. This gorgeous pendant is made up of pink and blue eye shapes around a circular coil. Glue on a pearl and you're done. Little ladies will love this project.

10. Quilled Toy Paper Tops

Quilling can even be used for toy making. Youngsters will be delighted with this paper leading craft. All you need to do is make a round paper coil for the bottom of the top, and after that construct a wall of paper to form the base.

11. Colorful Paper Flower Frame

Are you searching for an affordable but yet impressive gift to give to someone? This quilled paper frame might just be the best answer for you! Glue quilled flowers around a thrifty frame and you'll instantly have a gorgeous gift.

Chapter 4: Guide To Making Your Own Handmade Card Design, Bracelets and Other Through Quilling

Handcrafted cards typically come from an idea and materialize into an actual product. It usually starts with carving interesting shapes with scissors and then changing the material into an entirely different product altogether.

There are so many different colours, patterns, textures, and forms available for one to create handcrafted cards. Inspiration can come from many other craft hobbies such as origami, quilling, paper mâché, and pop-up storybooks.

Other inspirations for card designs stem from everyday surroundings outside in nature, through clothing styles and trends in fashion, and life experiences. Occasions can also be inspirational. Common events such as birthdays, weddings, showers, mother's day, father's day, and Christmas.

Once you get inspired to create a card, creativity is another difficult challenge to overcome. What materials to use and how to make it are the first things that come to mind. Determine what you have available and what you need. You already probably have the occasion in mind, so think about who you are actually making the card for. Reflect back on their personality and interest and add something to it you think they'll like. If it's a birthday, maybe make the theme one of their favourite hobbies. If it's a Christmas card, make the theme a winter sport they like. There are endless possibilities, that is why handcrafted cards can be so personal and custom.

As you become better at creating cards, you may branch out into the business of creating them for others and selling them. This industry continues to grow as personalization is a unique offering for those special occasions. However, practice your inspiration, ideas and creativity before venturing into this field. Understanding how what to use, how to use and what looks best is important in commercializing a handcrafted card business.

The following steps are methods to make the main shapes.

1. Firstly, place a wax paper sheet on your work surface. Then, remove a piece of quilling paper to the proper size like the project pattern.
2. Put the last part of quilling paper on the tool like a corsage pin.
3. To produce a circle shape, hold the paper with your thumb and forefinger. Next, twist it and turn the tool. It will wind up into a tight circle. Continue turning and construct a larger circle. Hold it and glue the ripped end to link it.
4. If you wish to produce a loose circle, cut the length of the material. Roll it to the tool and remove it.

5. To make a teardrop shape, you must turn the loose circle. Glue the end and hold the end with your thumb and forefinger. Then, squeeze the end to construct a teardrop shape.

6. For making a marquise shape, very first glue the end of the circle and hold it. Twist both ends to develop a marquise shape.

7. Meanwhile to make a square, roll a loose circle and glue the end. Pinch the both sides by turning the piece and turn two opposite locations to build the square.

8. You can start to make a teardrop shape and glue ending to form a triangle. Squeeze two points with thumb and forefinger to construct a triangle.

9. To develop a flower and patterns, simply glue shaped pieces together. You are permitted to select quilled pieces with tweezers.

Quilling Instructions For Quilling Craft Beginners

In the beginning, it is an excellent idea to use a slotted quilling tool as this will make things a bit much easier. As you grow in confidence and development you may want to change to using a needle or a toothpick.

One needs to carefully place the end of a quilling paper strip into the slot of the quilling tool. Ensure that you hold the quilling tool with the hand you use professionally and the paper should be held between your forefinger and thumb. Thoroughly and gradually in the beginning turn the quilling tool, winding the paper round the idea uniformly and with the edges level.

When you have actually rolled enough paper to make the size of coil you desire hold it for a minute or so, let go of the paper and tip the tool over to permit the paper coil to drop onto your work area. Do not get tense when the paper begins to unravel a little, this will always occur.

Before gluing the end of the paper coil, it is best to allow it to unwind and uncoil itself a little. When you are sure it has stopped use a cocktail stick or something comparable to put an extreme percentage of tacky glue onto the end of the paper and stick it into place.

Do not get stressed if your very first couple of coils are not best, it takes practice!

Once you have your coil shapes it is then time to pinch and squeeze them into the shapes you need to develop a picture.

Pro Quilling Tips Every Beginner Should Know

When you are learning to quill, it is natural for you to want your completed quilling to look precisely like the pattern you are following, however it most likely will not. There are lots of elements that affect the look of a quilled piece that a lot of artists are not even understanding. Here are five quilling pointers that discuss the issues you might be having and what you can do to create more constant, professional quillwork that you can be happy with.

Your scrolls and rolls will be special to you. They will not look exactly like mine or like those of anyone else. When they curl the paper strips resulting in variations in the scrolls and coils, everyone utilizes various tension. Not just that, but your own quills will differ from each other depending upon your state of mind and how you feel at the time. To see for yourself, compare coils that you made when you are tired out or exhausted with those made when you are unwinded and rested. You'll see a big distinction. A great tip is to prepare all of your strips for a task at one time. This permits you to roll your strips one right after the other, producing quills with more constant tension.

Neatness counts, control the glue. Absolutely nothing will ruin the appearance of a piece of finished quilling more than seeing little bits of glue all over it or gobs of glue under it where it is connected to its backing. It just takes the smallest drop to seal the end of a coil to itself or to attach one coil or scroll to another as you build your design. A bit more adhesive might be needed to attach the paper quilling to the box or frame back, but very little. When working with paper filigree and you'll desire to clean your hands before beginning on any quilling job, tidy hands are an absolute must. The very best quilling suggestion I've found to assist keep glue off the fingers is to keep a wet paper towel convenient to wipe your fingers on as you quill. Also, keep cold cream to a minimum so the oils don't tarnish the paper.

All quilling paper is not produced equal. You would think that one package of 1/8 inch wide paper would be the same as another, however that's not the case. As all of us understand, paper is available in different weights and even among those of the very same weight, some documents simply have more "body" than others making them more suitable for quilling. The weight of the paper used to produce the strips will differ somewhat between producers and even within the exact same maker. In fact, there is one producer out there offering quilling strips made from thin card stock that is very difficult to work with because it cracks and divides. If you are having a problem with quilling, before you quit out of aggravation, try a strip of paper from various businesses. You might find that the issue with your coils is with the paper and not you.

Quilling paper has a "right" and a "wrong" side. If you analyze a strip of quilling paper, you will observe that one side has smooth edges that curve down ever so somewhat. The opposite has edges that a little curve up. This is since the paper cutting blade lowers on the paper as it cuts. The smooth side is thought about the right (or top) side of the paper. You will want to start your curls with this side of the paper up. This distinction is especially visible when joining a number of strips together to form a large tight coil for usage as a base, and so on.

Use the quilling tool that works for you. There are numerous industrial tools readily available for curling paper, both straight and slotted needle types. A round toothpick or corsage pin can be used also.

Quilling tools are just that; tools to help you create the preferred coil or spiral. By all means, follow the directions that come with the tool or those you discover online, however if the instructions simply do not seem to work for you, do not hesitate to try using the tool in a slightly different method.

If you are still using a specific kind of tool, try a different tool completely. You will quickly find the one that is right for you.

Put these quilling suggestions to work for you and you'll see enhanced results in no time.

Chapter 5: Birthday Card Or Invitation

Card

You can make beautiful invitations in minutes with the kids, not only is it a fun and easy craft for kids, but it will save money as well. Plus. With just a few materials, you can make cards like these in minutes.

Materials needed to make party invitations

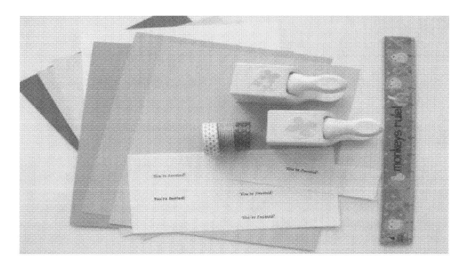

Gather the supplies you will need to make these cute party invitations. You will only need a few simple products to make these cute party invitations:

- Colored paper (you can use weight paper for text or, for a more paper-like appearance, use cardstock paper)

- Flower punch (any flower shape of your choice; these flowers were made with the hydrangea flower)
- Small dots of glue
- Ruler (you can use the ruler to give the cards a nice and neat fold)
- Scissors or paper cutters (to cut an 8 1/2 "x 11" sheet of paper in half and fold each half into a card)
- Washi tape
- Alternatively, use tissue paper flowers.

Steps:

1. **Use a paper punch to create flower shapes**

Make paper flower petals with your flower punch.

Next, take your paper flower piercings and make some paper flowers. (Note: you can use petals of the same size to stack on top of each other to create 3-dimensional flowers; however, using different-sized petals provides a more realistic look.)

2. Start making your own flowers

Use glue dots or a bead of glue to create your flower base.

Use a small dot of glue or a bead of glue to start assembling the base of your flower. Stack the main petals slightly flipped over the lower one so that the lower petals are visible.

3. Include more petals to finish your flower

Glue the rest of the petals together to form the flower. Add more petals of smaller size, using multi-colored paper for the smallest petal for the top center.

4. Here are some finished paper flowers

Your flowers will look like this.

Create lots of beautiful paper flowers in various colors. Place them on the celebration invitations and save the extra flowers in a box for later use. You can put these pretty paper flowers on thank you cards, birthday cards, celebration table placement cards, gift bags, or anything else you want to consider. The possibilities are limitless!

5. Include washi tape on your paper

Add some washi tape to your card and print or write the message on the front of the card.

Be sure to include the following information within your invitation to the celebration:

- Where (full address)
- Date (date and day of the week)
- Time (what time it ends and begins)
- RSVP information (your email and/or phone number).

Similarly, you may want to include any other information that visitors might need, such as how the children should dress, or the style of the party.

6. Timeless and fun outdoor party games

Produce multiple party invitations in a variety of colors. Interact with others to choose various colors of paper and washi tape patterns to produce a batch of party invitations. Let your creativity shine as you create beautiful cards in whatever you choose.

Chapter 6: Making Of Bracelets and

Necklaces

Most people are probably familiar with feathered flowers and leaves, however the method can also be used to develop beautiful, lightweight, and durable precious jewelry.

Yes, paper is a perfectly ideal product for earrings and bracelets, It is extraordinarily strong when rolled up and the finished parts can be further enhanced with fixative.

Styles made with rolled paper strips are getting more sophisticated which motivates people to try this awesome type of paper art.

To get an idea of how to roll jewelry paper, cut strips from a sheet of paper and roll them one at a time between your thumb and forefinger. With practice, the pressure. Some quillers don't use tools for measurement, they just depend on their fingers. However, most people crave to work with a needle tool or slit tool.

The needle tool takes longer to master, however the result will be a perfectly round bobbin. A superfine fluted tool is my favorite as it produces a little curl.

The materials used to make precious quilling jewelry include; paper strips and glue, they are simple and inexpensive to get.

Any type of glue suitable for paper will be ideal for quilling and you will be surprised how little is needed. My favorite gluing method is to put some clear adhesive gel on the lid of a plastic container. Since it does not affect skin when exposed to air, I prefer gel to white glue.

To prevent glue from blocking the tip as you work, place it upside down in a votive candle holder or cup lined with a damp paper cloth. A damp cloth is also useful for cleaning sticky fingers.

When the specific shapes of the pens are finished, arrange them with tweezers on a tray or corkboard and glue them one at a time. You can use pins to hold the shapes in place until the glue is dry. Flip the piece over to use featured glue dots on the seams and apply a light fixative when you finish if you prefer.

A clean Styrofoam tray is great for organizing and gluing feathered pieces. Last but not least, attach the results to the pieces.

Step 1: Material Required

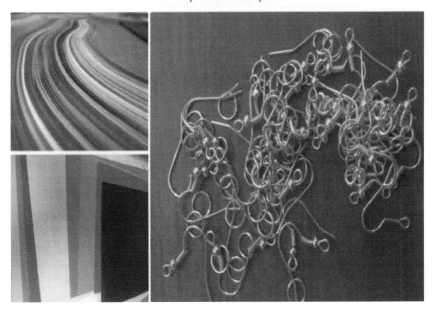

Step 2: How to Quill?

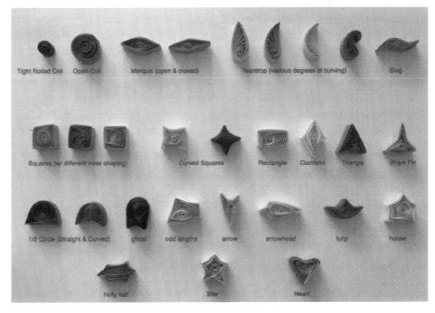

Step 3: To Begin With..

Step 4: Assemble Your Earrings

Step 5: Make. Wear. Flaunt.

Chapter 7: Wall Décor

Craft enthusiasts often think about how to make a stunning wall design using the quilling technique. The Art of Quilling includes many simple floral designs. When it comes to discovering a beginner-friendly Quilling style, leaves and flowers are the best choices you can make, in the middle of it all.

Quilling styles for wall frames should be attractive and have a beautiful look. Quilling art and colorful, elegant Quilling design are wonderful when handcrafted.

 Quilling, weaving, and shelling. All of these technical components combine to produce a fantastic coat rack that anyone with knowledge of the basic ways of quilling and shelling could make. The weaving is in basic patterns and the use of this intriguing technique adds dimension and depth.

The flowers are simple and eccentric marquises shapes, with yellow skins to accentuate. The leaves are shaped like a dark green and dark green marquise. Yellow accents are rolls of glue of various lengths, glued together.

Another type of wall hanging is the wreath. This popular hanging design works well for parties, as seasonal tags, and appears in almost any room in many homes. The bow is a simple collection of narrow strips, some loosely rolled to create a ribbon effect. The use of various types of flower making techniques brings additional interest to this design.

Wall hangings can be suspended within metal or wooden rings, using thread or tape to hold the piece in place. The feathers can be attached to the cord that is grasped and held tightly in a needle loop.

Any preparation for a wreath can have padded shapes glued to it, producing pieces that can reflect and spice up the holiday or your home area. And the designs are limited only by your imagination and the decision to create something that is yours alone.

We will go a step further with our flowers, developing independent designs that do not need paper support, the frame or the wall as support.

An important tool in these projects is florist wire, which can be gotten from artisan stores. If you cannot find such a thread, you can use a fairly light craft thread; just cover it with a green flower wrap or bandana to hide the metal.

The eccentric white marquise and the tears are used to imitate a basket, so that the cork seems to be the "foot" of it. The flowers are twisted pinks, small tufted flowers, and extremely small bunny ears with tight spiral centers. The leaves are cut and engraved. All shapes are mounted on wires and pressed in artisan polystyrene.

Let's take a look at how to make floral wall decorations use Quilling Art.

Materials needed:

- Thermocol Sheet
- Stairs

- Quilling strips

- Quilling needle

- Adhesive

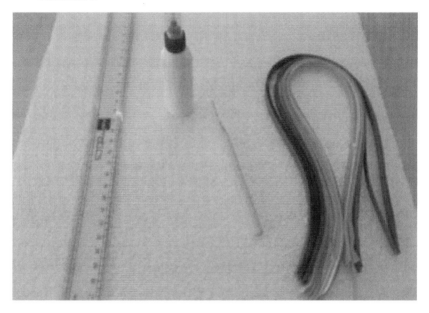

Steps:

1. Create the base

Take a sheet of thermocol and cut it to the size of 30 * centimeters on each side, giving you a square of thermocol.

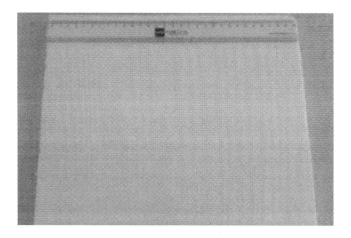

2. Let's make a double shadow filigree coil

Start by joining an orange stripe with 3-4 stripes to create a long double shadow Quilling stripe. This will give you a double shadow coil as shown in the picture.

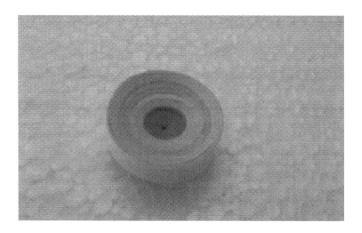

Take the quilling needle and make tight coils with it and secure the end of the coil with glue. Lightly push the starter coils to get a styling coil as shown above. Put it in the center of the sheet and stick it with glue.

3. Make more quilling coils

Take some yellow quilling strips and make numerous narrow coils from each one. Make some big and some small.

4. Start creating the Design

Now take the orange strip and stick it with the adhesive, keeping the quilling strip vertical. Attach a yellow spiral to the end of the petal.

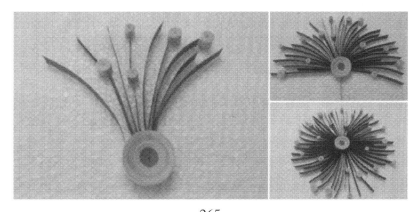

Place a second, smaller petal next to the first, using the same method. Make the floral pattern in such a way that all of your petals appear consistent even after being of different sizes.

Strategically glue the narrow yellow spirals in the middle, to provide the designer with the Quilling pattern.

5. Create leaves for the flower

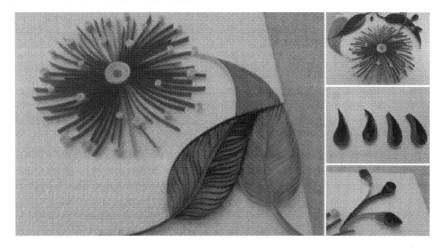

Now start with the leaf. With the help of your finger, fold and fold the green Quilling strip into a leaf shape.

Attach it in the same way, vertically, as you did with the flower.

After applying the pan, cut different sizes of green Quilling strips accordingly, to give the leaf veins a realistic look. Use sap green and dark green for a richer look.

6. Give it a final touch

In the end, make some tight and loose orange coils and edge the sheet with a thermal neck to provide more information to the Quilling design.

7. Your creation is ready!

And that is it! A stunning wall decor with handcrafted Quilling art and handmade by you. It just takes a little patience to make this lovely Quilling-style wall frame, but the effort is definitely worth the wait.

Make this Quilling art style a part of your home design and watch the world in awe of your talent!

Chapter 8: Types Of Quilling Patterns And Project Ideas

If you are completely new to quilling, try these simple quilling ideas.

1. Quilling narrow circles

One of the easiest quilling designs to create is a simple, tight circle, secured in place with a glue. This shape is produced by inserting quilling strips into the slotted end of a quilling tool, then wrapping the strips around the tool before removing it.

2. Quilling loose circles

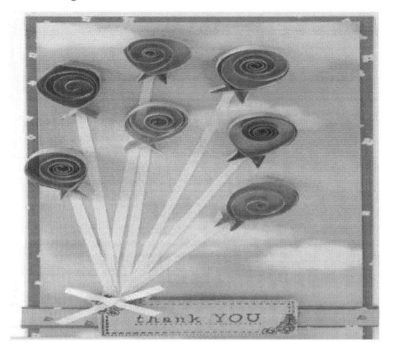

To produce these fun feathered balloons, simply start to develop a tight circle with feathers, as in the previous work, but instead of gluing the ends together, let the tension in the circle loosen slightly, to reveal a swirling circular design. , before gluing the free end. instead. Squeeze one end of the balloon a little to give it more shape, then whistle a small strip of paper and glue it to the pinched end. Also include thin strips of paper to represent the strings of the balloons.

3. Quilling teardrops

This flexible shape can be used for many different styles. You can use it to develop leaves on this cute wreath card. To develop the shape, simply pinch the glued end of a loose circle to form a point.

4. Quilling squares and hearts

To create the square cake tiers on this wedding card, pinch two opposite sides of a circle with loose feathers into points, rotate the pinched circle 90 degrees, and then pinch two more points on the remaining rounded sides. To make the sweet feathered hearts, fold a quilling strip in half, unfold it to form a "V," then curl the ends inward.

5. Diamond quilling

To get the diamond shape, simply make a quilted square, then apply light pressure to two opposite corners. You can mix teardrop and diamond shapes to create a quilted floral embellishment for a label.

6. Quilling rolls

Similar to heart designs, you can form the ends of a folded quilling strip so that they curve outward. The flower heads were formed by surrounding a small loose circle with rings of quilling strips.

7. Quilling lockets and earrings

Just like quilling on cards, you can also make some amazing quilling jewelry, like this quilling pendant. Start by cutting a shape out of paper, then drape a strip of quilling paper several times around the outside. Make a range of small loose circles in different colors, to fit the shape, then include the 3D glitter on top to seal it in.

8. How to quill your A, B, C

From abstract patterns to intricate wildlife designs and fairy tales, let your creativity run free. Draw the selected letter and carefully glue the edge of the quilling strips around it. Surround the letter with your choice of quilt shapes to develop this colorful decoration.

9. Let your creativity fly with feathered birds

Use quilted shapes to develop characters on your cards, such as birds or other wild animals. This stunning flamingo is made up of a series of loose circles and tears in different sizes, as well as strips of quilling paper folded lengthwise for the neck and legs. You can pair the quilted flamingo with our fabulous tropical bird pattern cards.

10. Quilling greeting Cards

Start writing greetings with the scrolling technique. Write your choice in pencil initially, then cut strips of quilling paper, curl the ends, and glue it in place along the edges.

11. Quilling snowflakes

12. Quilling vase

Spice up an old vase with these ombre paper drops.

13. Quilling of hearts

Write your design and then glue it to paper for a gift or frame it for your wall.

14. Quilling for Christmas

15. Quilling frames

16. Acorn quilling

Chapter 9: Photo Frame

A great and simple way to spend lots of time with your children and help them contribute to a home improvement task. The photo frame looks lovely as a mantelpiece and even as a gift.

Required materials:

- Cardboard, paper or cardboard, color of your choice

- Scale / ruler

- Paper cutter

- Eraser

- Pencil

- Glue

- Handmade paper / expensive paper

- Quilled Flowers

- And a lot of illusion!

Steps:

1. Cut the front and back pieces of paper

Mark 7 inches wide and 6 inches tall on the paper card, using a pencil and a scale / rule.

Cut the paper with the help of a letter opener, it is best to ask your children to mark the size and you cut it. You will need 2 of these pieces of paper, for the back and front of the photo frame.

Since we are making enough frame for the size of a 4 x 3 inch image, we will need to cut a window out of one of the sheets of paper. Now, to be exceptionally accurate, you'll need to make sure your window is in the center of the sheet of paper.

Create an area using the 4 sided scale / ruler to create the points of a 4 inch x 3 inch rectangular shape for your window. Use the cutter and scale / ruler to help you better cut the required rectangle.

2. Cover the pieces of paper with patterned paper

Once the front window and back cover card stock are ready, we need to cover it with fancy paper or craft paper of your choice. To cover the back of the picture frame, use glue gently to stick the expensive paper onto the sheet of paper. Now to make sure the card is fully covered, make sure your fancy card is larger than your sheet of paper. Use the gift wrap approach as an envelope to cover the piece.

For the front of the sheet of paper, use expensive, light-colored paper. Put the front of the frame on the patterned paper and just one inch larger than our frame. Please mark a square smaller than our window in the picture frame and cut out the paper. Make grooves at all four corners and inside the patterned paper so that it is folded and adhered to the frame. Apply the glue generously and you now have both the front and back of the picture frame in place.

3. Bring the front and back of the photo frame together

Glue the 2 pieces of the front and back frame now ready. Please note that you need to glue only 3 sides and leave one side open, so you can move on to the photo of your choice.

4. Decorate the photo frame

Quilted flowers and leaves produce colorful decorations.

These can be used to decorate anything, straight from paper bags, gift bags, boxes, and of course, photo frames.

Use a variety of padded flowers and leaves to produce a few bunches to spruce up your frame. Now what I've actually done is use the corners of my image frame to accentuate the look, but you can completely hide the sides of the frame to your liking.

To make the backing, use cardstock or cardstock, glue it to a larger sheet, and fold. It depends on whether you want your frame to be vertical or horizontal. Conveniently, you will need to glue the bracket to the frame.

Hope you enjoy quilling and item crafting with your family and friends.

Chapter 10: Teardrop Vase

This stylish quilled teardrop vase is an amazing project for starting quillers. Just glue teardrop shapes in gradients of color onto a vase. This job can be made in under an hour. Who does not love a craft job that's simple and fast, but still looks so upscale.

Changing paper rolls into quilling shapes is as simple as pinching one or more sides.

How many sides are pinched, and how close these sides are, is what identifies the end result. Tearsdrop are a great place to start handling quilling shapes, because they are simply a matter of gently squeezing one side of the loose coil. Some shapes even have slight variations.

Steps:

1. **Fold the tip of your teardrop between your fingers and you have created a shaped teardrop**

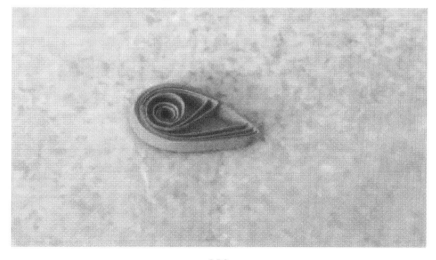

2. Tears are the best sheets or starting point for these quilling paper snowflakes

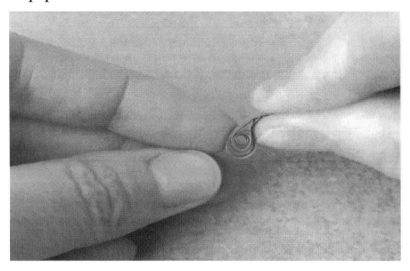

3. Pinch two opposite ends of a loose spiral at the same time to develop a marquise

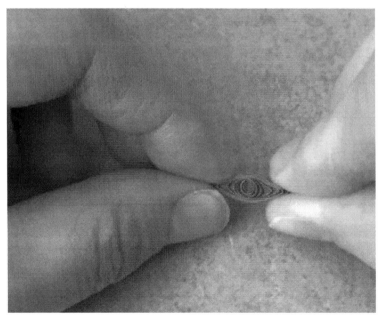

As in the case of the shaped teardrop, flexing the marquise will form a new shape!

4. **This time, use both hands to press and flex the marquise tips into an "S" shape.** It is shaped like a marquise.

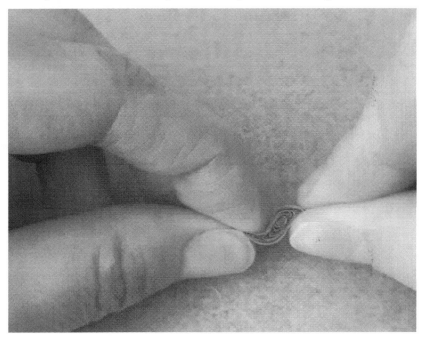

5. **Again, starting with a loose coil, pinch both sides, but keep the bottom flat with your thumbs at the same time**

The semicircles were the shapes I used to form my white paper lilacs!

This may take a couple of sessions, however you can!

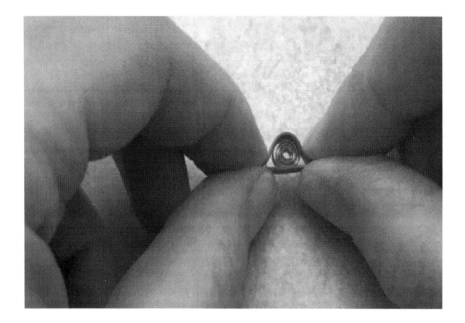

6. From a semicircle you can create a half moon

It is as simple as folding the center of the moon over your thumb.

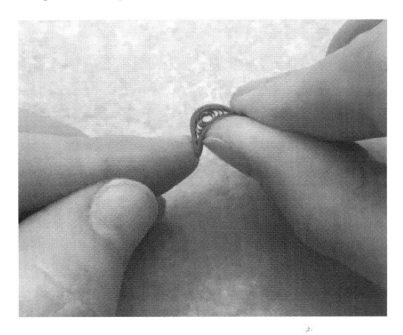

After reviewing some of these new shapes, start tweaking them a bit.

7. Instead of flexing your fingertips, you could possibly use a wooden dowel. When you pinch the center of the coils a bit, notice how they look. I bet you will quickly develop really special and natural shapes!

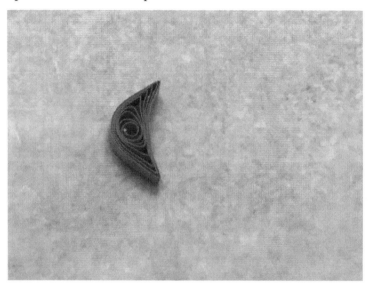

Chapter 11: Bats

Why not surprise your kids with these intriguing Halloween crafts and have a lovely time together making paper quilled crafts? This Paper Quilled bat craft is extremely enjoyable.

What you need:

- Quilling paper: you can quickly buy it online. You need 3 strips of black paper.
- A quilling tool
- A toothpick: this is the very best way to apply the glue
- Tacky glue
- A ruler: to determine the strip lengths that you need. After some experience, you'll be able to eyeball this
- 2 earring wires
- 2 dive rings - I didn't have any on hand so I made my own with some wire
- Little needle/nosed pliers: for connecting the earring wires and leap rings
- Quilling form *(optional)*: It is not absolutely necessary as you can merely form the coils and size them without it but you might discover it convenient when you begin doing bigger, more elaborate projects.

Steps:

1. **Take a 20 inch long (or longer) quilling strip and use the slotted quilling tool to coil the entire strip.** Get the coil from the tool and allow the coil to loosen up freely. As soon as you are pleased with the coil size, glue the open end of the coil to protect it. Now glue the loose coil on a piece of dark color craft paper; I use grey.

2. **Carefully cut the craft paper all around the coils' outer edge**

Take a 10-inch long quilling strip and produce a loose coil pattern with it

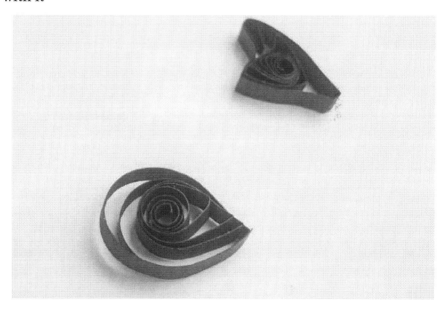

3. Press any one side of the loose coil to form a teardrop shape

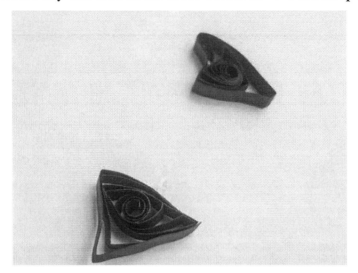

4. Now press 2 more sides (on the opposite side of the formerly pushed location) of the teardrop; this will form a triangular shape

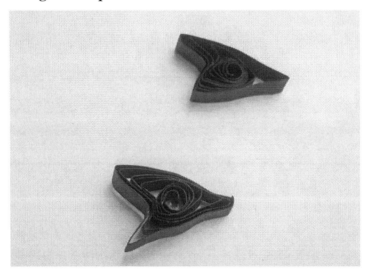

5. **Now press and fold in the middle part of any two pressed sides of the triangular shape.** Similarly, create another one of these patterns. These 2 will be the wings of the bat; you will need to create 2 more shapes for the wing.

6. **Take 5 inches long quilling strip and form a triangular shape. Likewise, develop another one.** These 2 will be the ears of the bat.

7. Use a 5-inch quilling strip to produce 2 lens shapes, 4-inch quilling strips to develop 2 lens shapes and 2-inch quilling strips to create 2 loose coils. The 2 sets of lens shapes are for the wings and the 2 loose coils will be the legs.

8. Place the ready items on a flat surface to examine the bat pattern

9. Combine the prepared parts one by one by using craft glue

10. **Cut out the eyes, mouth and, fangs of the bat.** Merely use white craft paper to eliminate the eyes and the fangs. Use a black sharpie to draw the eyeballs and use a pink craft paper for the mouth.

11. **Stick the prepared parts on the big loose coil pattern. Enable the glue to dry entirely.** And, done!

Chapter 12: Paper Quilled Monogram

With time, practice and a little persistence, you will soon end up being a professional.

Materials:

- Pair of scissors
- Handcrafted paper knife
- Tweezers
- Adhesive glue
- 1 old paper plate or plastic glue container
- Brush
- Pre-cut cardboard or quilling strips in the desired colors
- 1 sheet of thick cardboard or cardboard for the background
- 1 Shadowbox photo frame.

Steps:

1. **Print your Strip.** Print your chosen letter, filled with a light or dark colored background of your choice, on the background of the cardstock

Alternative methods to create letters

If you don't have access to a printer, use this alternative technique for a letter:

i. Trace a large character from a character, such as a book or a magazine, onto a sheet of paper using a pencil.

ii. Use a light touch with the pencil, you don't want to see the pencil lines on your project. It will be difficult to remove the lines after building the frame.

iii. Or you can filled the letter with a favorite background color peeking out from under the covered pieces.

iv. Use a ruler to make the lines straight.

v. Attach the tracing paper to a card for stability, if desired.

2. Cut the strips:

i. Choose the card in the colors you want to integrate into your style.

ii. Use the cutter to cut 1/4 inch wide strips of paper from card stock.

...or buy pre-cut cardboard strips:

Instead of cutting strips, purchase pre-cut quilling paper packets online or at the craft store.

3. **Give the stripes a shape.** When choosing what your letter's interior design will be, it's time to create shapes.

i. Take a strip of paper and wrap it around the toothpick or quilling tool in any way you like, rolled tightly (for a compact shape) or loose, whichever way you prefer.

ii. Put some glue on the end of the paper strip to hold the shape in place.

iii. Before curling the stripes, take a look at other feathered monograms for inspiration and make a quick miniature initial sketch for your monogram design.

Six Common Types of Rolled Quilling Shapes

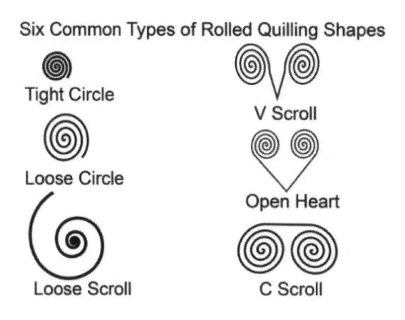

4. **Outline your letter with strips of paper.** Use your preferred method of applying glue to the pieces of paper that will form the frame of your letter.

Glue: less is better.

Too much glue can destroy your work, so be careful. There are two ways to apply glue to the straight strips of paper that make up the letter frame. Use one of these techniques to place your feathered and shaped pieces inside the letter frame as well:

i. Use a light touch and a small brush to apply the glue to the edge of the paper.

ii. Gently place the strips on a glued paper plate to lightly cover the edge of a piece, then arrange the pan.

5. Frame the outside of the letter with strips of paper:

i. Glue and place your strips in the outline of your letter. Gently hold each strip until the glue is solid enough to allow the paper strip to rise on its own.

ii. Make a neat fold in a strip of paper and attach a drop of glue to each end and overlap each corner. This little strip will set the corners.

iii. Glue and overlap a quarter-inch strip as an anchor anywhere else you join with a strip of paper that creates the wall. The layers will make the frame more powerful.

iv. Let the pen wall dry completely for writing.

6. **Start filling in the frame of your letter.** As soon as you've built the outdoor frame, fill the inside with your monogram.

i. Follow your style and glue the shapes and strips into place, using your fingers and tweezers for tight spaces.

ii. Allow the finished piece to dry completely for a few hours.

7. **Use your tweezers.** Tweezers are a quiller's best friend. They are one of the most important tools you will use because they help you place paper shapes of all sizes in small spaces within your monogram work without interrupting the frame.

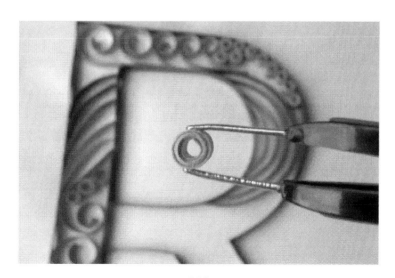

8. Frame the monogram with the finished quill. When your piece is dry, place it in the frame of your shadow box.

The importance of a Shadowbox framework

A base frame with glass is not deep enough to accommodate your feathered monogram. You will need a shadow box at least an inch deep to accommodate the raised surface of the pen activity.

Chapter 13: Paper Quilled Teardrop Vase

What you will need:

- A vase: Preferably a ceramic vase in a simple way, which worked very well. We need an opaque vase, not too big, that does not have severe curves, but soft and gentle curves

- Paper Strips in a Gradient Color - Search online or visit a paper craft store and you will find paper strip sets at an affordable price in a wide range of colors. You will only need one set for a small vase like mine

- Glue: must have the ability to glue the paper to the ceramic

- Grooved Quilling Tool: This is a rod with a groove at the end essentially and it's cheap to buy

- Quilling Needle Tool: You can instead use a cocktail stick or anything with a tip that can apply glue correctly

- Quilling board *(optional)* - Very convenient to have to make sure the tears are the same size. However, you could use a ruler or just draw a circle on paper to use as a guide

- Convenient to have: tweezers to move difficult objects and a cotton swab to clean glue on the go.

Steps:

1. Roll up the paper spirals

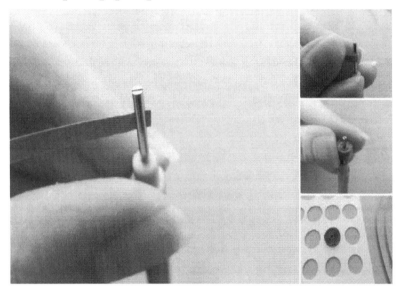

- Starting with the darkest paper color to use, place the end of a paper strip in the slitting tool.

- You want to rotate the tool by holding the paper strip so that the paper wraps tightly around the metal rod.

- It's not critical, however, the paper strips have a smoother side and a rougher side, so try to keep the smoother side on the outside of the spiral.

- While rotating the tool, hold the forming reel with your finger to check it and prevent it from becoming loose or dirty.

- Place the bobbin in a circle on the quilling board and let it slowly unfold to fill the hole-shaped guide after turning the entire strip into a bobbin. I used the third hole down, which is 17mm in diameter.

- If you don't have a quilling board, you can use a drawn circular guide or ruler and let the coil loosen until it reaches the desired size.
- Then you need to put some glue on the end of the paper strip, inside, to hold the spool due to its shape. You can use a quilling needle or cocktail to apply the glue accurately.

2. Form the tears

- You have to take each of the coils you make and then turn them into a teardrop shape.
- This is really easy and all you have to do is gently squeeze the centre of the coil between your index finger and thumb and pinch one end to create a sharp crease.

313

- It depends on you what size you make your tears and it mainly depends on the size of your vase. I made 4 rows of one size and then made smaller size tears for the top row.

3. Add the tears to the jar

- Make a handful of feathered tears to start. Then start gluing them to your vase, starting from the base.

- Just use some glue on the back (mainly the top and bottom) and hold the tear on the surface of the jar for a moment. It should stick pretty fast.

- When you have finished a row, you can duplicate all the steps with a different color and create the next row. And after that, duplicate all of this on your vase or until you don't want the design to be completed.

4. Finished!

In fact, you have now finished your beautiful feathered vase!

Chapter 14: Paper Quilled Flower Cake

Quilling simply involves winding paper ribbons into decorative shapes to produce an intricate 3-D resulting pattern. And as you might have thought, any pattern that can be produced with strips of paper can just as much be created with strips of gum paste or modeling paste and used in cake design.

You can even include more rolled strips to make these flowers look "fuller."

To make these feathered flowers, you will need the following supplies:

OPTION ONE

- Red gum paste or 50/50.
- Light blue or 50/50 gum paste.
- Yellow or 50/50 gum paste.
- Paint brush.
- Water.
- Embossing mat.
- Circle cutter.
- Pizza cutter or strip cutter.
- Roller.

Steps:

1. **Start rolling red and light blue or 50/50 gum paste**

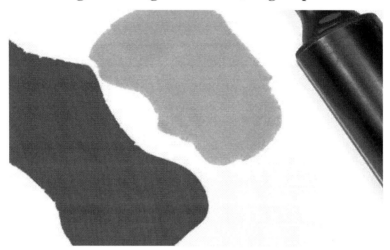

2. **Use a pizza cutter or fondant strip cutter to remove numerous strips.** My strips were half an inch wide and about 3 inches long

3. Brush some water onto one end of the strip only

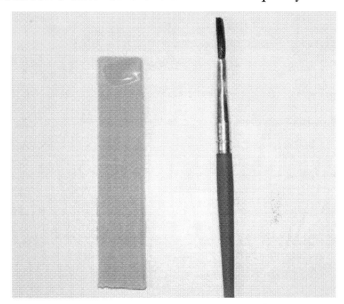

4. Fold the strip in a loop upward until both ends stick together

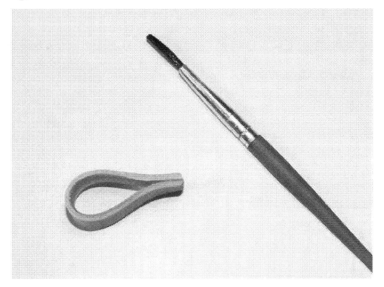

5. Repeat steps 3 and 4 for all remaining strips

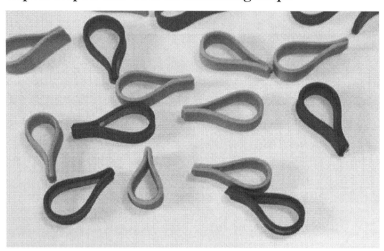

6. **Now, spread on some yellow or 50/50 gumpaste.** Lay an embossing mat on top and press up firmly until the pattern transfers to the gum paste.

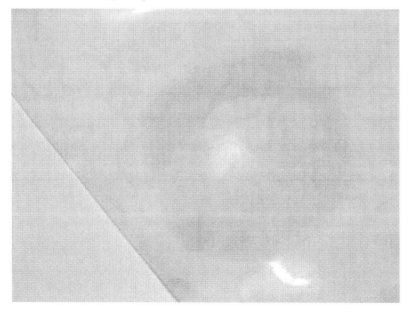

7. **Use a circular cutter to remove some pieces.** Each flower will need 2 of these circular pieces.

8. **Flip one of the circular pieces over so that the raised side is facing down.** Brush some water all over this piece.

9. Set all the blue and red ties around the circle

10. Brush some water onto another circular piece and glue it on
    top of the loops

You can also glue a lollipop stick through these flowers with some gumpaste glue or melted chocolate if you like. Then allow these pieces to dry overnight or until set and use on your cakes and cupcakes.

OPTION TWO

Materials:

- White printer paper
- Yellow paper
- Glue stick
- Scissors and / or paper cutter.

Steps:

1. For a fringed center, cut a piece of yellow cardstock (1.5cm X 3cm) and border the edge. Roll it up and protect it with a little glue

2. For flower petals, cut 1/4 " strips of printer paper

3. Roll the strip into a tight coil, let it unwind a bit, and secure it with a little glue

4. With 2 fingers, pinch the circular coil at the ends so that the shape ends up being more of a diamond

5. Keep making the diamond shapes until you have enough petals

6. To make a double diamond petal, make two diamond coils and flatten them, protecting them by wrapping another strip of paper around the outer edge of the two pieces and gluing them in place

7. Glue all the finished petals around the rolled or fringed centerpiece.

Chapter 15: Paper Quilling Flower Pendant

If you just love creating different and unconventional fashion jewelry, try this paper flower pendant. It's amazing and easy to do, you don't need to know how to make fancy jewelry to try it on!

Paper quilling is a fun hobby, and supplies are so cheap! You can use purchased quilling strips or make your own, you want to keep a texture and therefore it can be boring.

Once you're done making this paper flower pendant, try it out with other styles. Make it into a keyring, make smaller versions like earrings, and combine a few quilt patterns to make an eye-catching necklace or bracelet.

What you need to make a paper quilling flower pendant:

- Quilling paper strips
- Glue
- Crevice tool for quilling
- Jump ring
- Chain or full cord

  Optional:

- additional beads to decorate the chain.
- 4mm synthetic pearl

Steps:

1. Select a strip of paper in your first color and use the watermark tool to wrap the strip

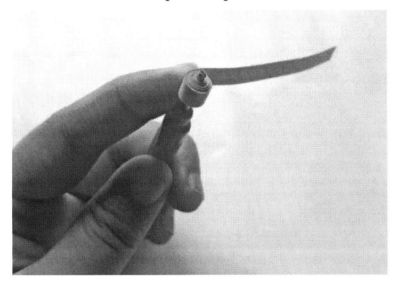

2. After tightly wrapping the entire strip, remove it from the quilling tool, holding the strip so that it does not unroll

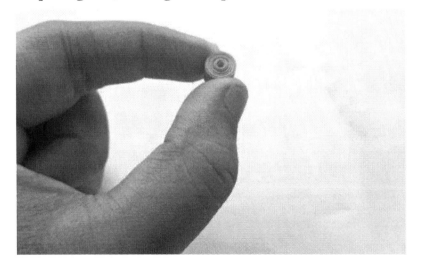

3. Let the coil loosen up

4. Lay the spiral strip on a flat surface and glue a small bead to the center of the quilted circle *(optional)*

5. **Retighten the coil by holding it between 2 fingers and pulling the open end.** As soon as the core has tightened, wrap the rest of the strip around and apply glue to the tip to protect the coil. This will be the center of the paper quilling flower

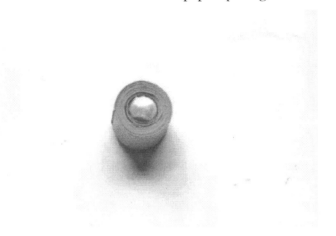

6. **Select a quilling strip in the second color and apply it using the slit quilling tool**

7. After quilling the strip, carefully remove it from the tool

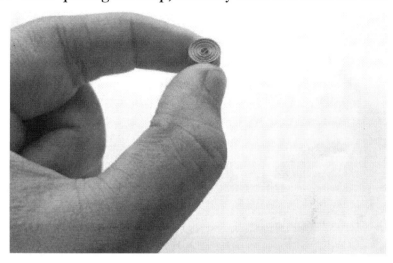

8. Allow the coil to loosen slightly by placing it on a flat surface

9. **Take the pattern loose and pinch one side to get a pointed edge.** You are now teardrop-shaped

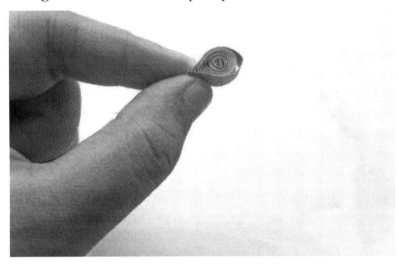

10. Now pinch the opposite side of the strip with the pen to develop another sharp edge. You are now having a shape like teardrop

11. **Repeat actions 6-10 to develop 5 more teardrop shapes using the identical colored strips for a total of 6.** Make 3 more shapes on the third color of the paper

12. **Get a notepad or plastic with a smooth surface** (so you can easily remove the glued pieces). Place the central part of the flower on its surface. Take the first 2 shapes of your color of which you have six and join them in the circle. Do this by gluing any of the pointed edges to the center circle. Also glue the rounded part of the eye shapes together, joining their petals together

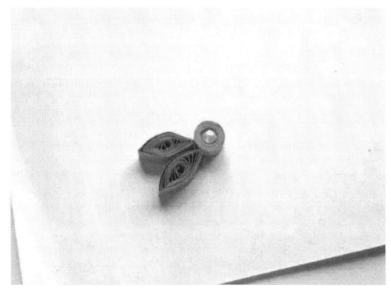

13. Now take one of your second color of the shaped swirls and glue it the same way in the center and on the adjacent petal

14. Repeat the pattern until the shape of the paper quilling flower is complete

15. Develop a narrow coil with a relatively larger ring in the center

16. Attach the spiral to the floral pattern between two of your petals to make it circulate. If you want to print your design, now is the time to do it. Make sure you leave the hole in the coil you made in step 15 open.

17. **Place a diving ring through the coil ring to complete the pendant**

18. **Attach your jump ring to a cable or chain and wear it with pride.** If you want to add beads, you will need to finish your chain or remove the accompanying endings and choose large beads with holes as accents

Wear it and be proud of your paper flower skills!

How to make a purple quilling paper flower necklace with decorated white pearls

Now let's see how to make the purple quilling paper flower necklace with decorated white pearls.

Materials needed:

- Quilling paper strip set
- 10mm White Round Pearl Beads
- 8mm white round pearl beads
- 6mm white round pearl beads
- Round flat white pearl cabochons
- Iron cross chains
- Silver jump rings
- Silver brooches
- Silver eyepins
- Round magnetic clasps in silver 11.5 x 6 mm
- Needle pliers
- Round nose pliers
- Rotating pen
- Tweezers
- White glue.

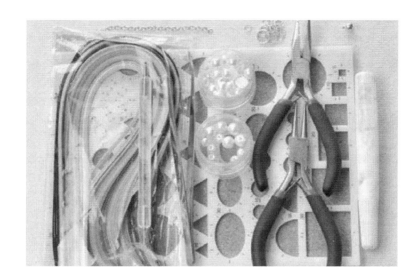

Steps:

1. Make the first part of the purple quilling paper flower pendant

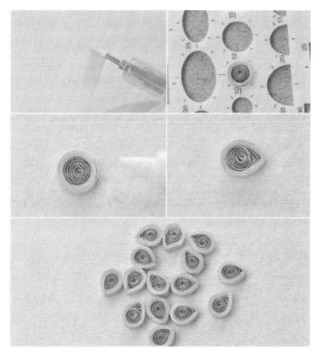

First, cut a piece of purple quilling paper and use the rolling pin to create a circular pattern.

Use white glue to fix the circular pattern and glue the endings.

Transform the circular motif into a teardrop motif.

Use white glue to combine 5 patterns of purple drops into one flower.

Use white glue to glue a flat round pearl white cabochon in the middle of the three purple quilling paper flowers respectively.

2. Make the remaining part of the purple quilling paper flower pendant

First, it integrates a 10mm white round pearl, 3 8mm white round pearls and 5 6mm white round pearls with the silver clips one by one.

Circle the other end of the silver pins. Combine 3 6mm white round beads with 3 8mm white round beads. Combine two 6mm white round beads together.

Refer to step 1 to make 7 more purple circular quilling paper patterns.

Add a purple circular quilling paper pattern on both sides of a purple quilling paper flower. Repeat this step as soon as possible. Include the other three purple circular quilling paper patterns in the other purple quilling paper flower.

Put the 10mm white round bead into the purple circular quilling paper pattern hole through a silver jump ring. Add the other 2 purple quilling paper flowers and 2 6mm round white beads through the silver rings (as shown in the picture).

3. Make the rest part of the purple quilling paper flower medallion

Add the 6 white round bead pattern to the hole of the other purple circular pattern through a silver dive ring. Cut 2 pieces of silver braided chain (approximately the same length) and include them on the two sides respectively.

Attach the two ends of the purple quilling paper flower locket via a 11.5 x 6mm silver round magnetic clasp and 2 silver dip rings.

Here is the latest appearance of the purple quilling paper flower necklace.

Chapter 16: Paper Quilling Snowflakes

Bring the fun of snow into your home with these simple paper snowflake accessories.

Feathered snowflakes can vary in style dramatically. Some are extremely comprehensive and remarkable, others are more basic.

They can really be done with the more standard quilling shapes.

The tricks are to use proportions in your designs and to keep the shape sizes consistent throughout the snowflake.

Materials:

- A blank sheet of A4 paper (the one you use for printing)
- Fluted quilling tool

- White glue and brush

- Scissors or utility knife

- Pencil

- Rule.

Steps:

1. Make the strips

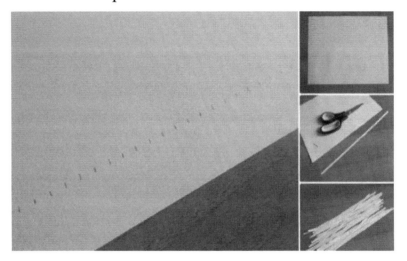

The first thing to do is divide the sheet of paper into strips. The strips should be 0.19 inches (0.5 cm) wide and as long as the longest side of the sheet of paper. It is very important that all the strips are the same width, so use a pencil and a ruler to do this.

When you have finished making all your strips, you should cut them.

Realizing that it would be much faster, I started to cut them with scissors, but after the first strip I used a cutter! Try to be as many as possible in this step.

2. The first reel

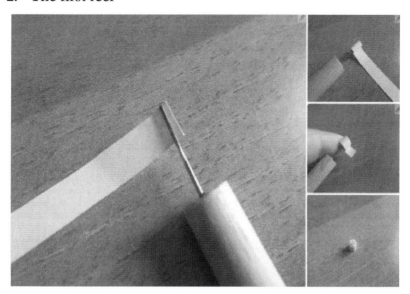

Let's start with the coils!

Take between the strips you just cut and insert between their ends in the quilling tool.

Begin rotating the tool making sure the paper is taut and continue rotating until you reach the other end of the strip.

When you do, remove the paper roll from the tool and tape the end to secure it.

Your first reel is ready!

This will be the centre of the snowflake.

3. The tears

Now you need to make another coil like this but before gluing it to close it, release it a little between your fingers so that it is not as tight as the first (loose coil).

Secure it with glue. We will not leave this reel this time.

Press it on one side with your thumb and forefinger to create a teardrop shape. Now do 5 more pieces, for a total of 6.

Glue the tip of the teardrop around the first coil you made, using white glue.

You will get a shape that will remind you of a flower.

4. The eyes

Make 6 loosed coils.

We will provide a new way now. Instead of pressing it only on one side, you need to press the coil with both hands at the same time so that the coil becomes more like an oval. This is called an eye.

Make 6 eyes like this and glue them between the petals of the "flower" you made earlier.

5. Smaller coils

Now cut 3 strips in half to get 6 strips.

With these shorter strips you need to make 6 narrow coils, similar to the first one you made. The only difference is that they will end up being smaller, of course.

6. The first snowflake

Glue the smaller coils to the tips of the "eyes" you made in step 4, always using white glue.

Since these shapes are so small and round, you need to press them down a bit to make sure they stick together.

This is already a good snowflake!

If you want to keep it that way, skip the following steps and go to step 9.

7. **More loose coils**

Now make 6 regular loose spirals and glue them on the tears, between the eyes.

8. The squares

Let's create a new shape now. Roll out 6 looser coils and secure with glue. Shaping them with the fingertips to get a square. You have to press on 2 sides as you did with your eyes, then push the coil in to develop 2 more angles. Rotate it to change it.

Glue the edge of the squares to the large loose coils you created in step 7.

9. You need a coil with a hole in the center to be able to hang the snowflake

To do this, use a thin cylinder (I used the handle of my quilling tool, a round pencil would work too) and twist a strip around like you did the other coils. The only difference is that instead of gluing the paper only at the end, I also glued it at the beginning, to make sure that the paper forms a circle that doesn't move inward.

Glue this piece to one of the tight coils of your snowflake.

You can also apply a little clear varnish over the entire surface to make your design shiny and more durable if you prefer.

String a thread through the hole and you're ready to hang your snowflake on your Christmas tree!

ANOTHER METHOD

Follow our easy instructions to fold and cut paper into distinctive, eye-catching paper snowflakes.

Materials needed:

- Paper (preferably thin or light paper)

- Pair of scissors

- Conveyor *(optional)*.

Steps:

1. Make a square out of paper

Start with a square, light, or preferably thin sheet of paper. You can use square origami paper or follow these simple actions to make a square out of any rectangular paper.

2. Fold in half diagonally

3. Fold the square diagonally in half to form a triangle

Fold the resulting triangle in half to make a smaller triangle.

4. Divide the triangle into 3 sections

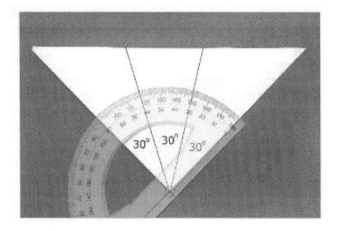

The most crucial and perhaps the most complicated step in creating a paper snowflake is dividing the triangle into three equivalent sections. The most accurate way to do this is to use a protractor to divide the angle at the vertex of the triangle (the angle opposite the longest side) into three areas, each at a 30-degree angle. If you don't have a protractor, you can approximate the size of the areas by following steps 5 and 6.

5. Fold the left section

Fold the left section forward as soon as you have marked the 3 equivalent sections.

6. Fold the right section

Fold the ideal section forward.

7. Rotate the shape

Flip the shape over so the side with the horizontal edge meets the front.

8. Cut along the horizontal edge

Cut along the horizontal edge to make a wedge.

9. Cut out random shapes

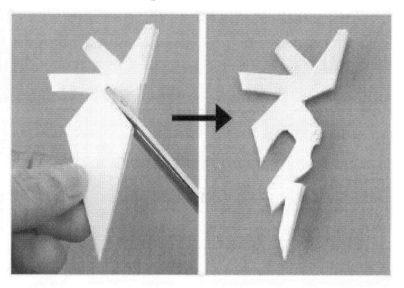

Keeping the wedge bent, cut random shapes from the edges.

If you are looking to find ready-to-cut snowflake patterns, you can find them online.

.

10. Open the card

Open the paper completely to reveal your paper snowflake. Like real snowflakes, your paper snowflake has a 6-pointed or 6-sided balance.

11. Create more snowflakes

In nature, no two snowflakes are exactly alike. Try editing the shape cutouts in step 9 to create your own unique snowflakes.

Chapter 17: Paper Quilling

Watermelon Jewelry

Watermelon pendant

Materials:

- 5mm filigree strips in red, white, light green and dark green or Glue

- Holder for pendants (rings)

- Filigree needle

- Black marker.

How to make your own watermelon pendant with the duvet

Steps:

1. **Create a narrow bobbin using 15 strips of red quilling**

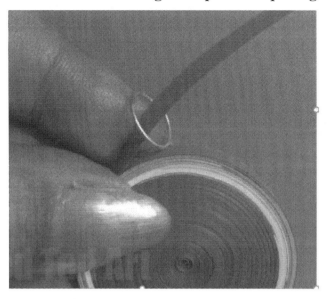

2. **Take 2 strips of white quilling and wrap them around the narrow red bobbin.** Take 2 strips of light green quilling and repeat the same procedure, except on the white color.

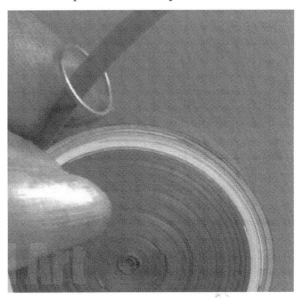

3. **Continue the process of the dark green strips to, keep in mind that as you cover it around the light green color, after one round of wrapping, put a pendant to hang across the strip and continue wrapping.** Whenever you reach the pendant holder, pass the quilling strip through it and not over it. As soon as it is complete, glue the end of the paper.

4. **With a black marker, draw small dots all over the red spool and voila! Your watermelon feather pendant is ready!**

Chapter 18: Paper Quilling Frequently Asked Questions

- **What is Quilling?**

Quilling is an ancient art form whose roots are to be discovered in the Middle East, it is probably in Ancient Egypt where we should find its noble origins. It is an art type that involves the use of hand-rolled, shaped and glued strips of paper to develop decorative styles. There are lots of shapes and methods that can be utilized in Quilling art. The most utilized shapes are: the circle, the drop, the eye, the triangle, the square, the leaf, the crescent, the star, the arrow and the tulip. Rather the most used techniques are: Quilling Comb (Comb Technique), Quilling Beheeve (Beehive Technique), Husking Technique, Quilling Edge and quilling comb.

- **What are the creations made of?**

The material mostly used to make such creations is PAPER. When it involves 3D items and bijoux, the paper is treated with non-toxic water-based paint for shock and wetness resistance.

- **What type of card do you use? What is the weight of the quilling paper?**

For my quilling jobs I use a large choice of colored papers and cards. In particular, I use Fabriano, Favini, Canson paper and great papers of different weights. The paper weight differs according to the quilling job I have to make. I use weights from 80 g/ m2, 120 g/ m2 and up to 220 g/ m2 for paper strips.

- **Can I create quilling painting?**

Yup! You have the ability to recreate a quilling painting. However it will not be precisely similar due to the qualities of a handmade craft product, however it will be really comparable.

- **Can I make any type of quilling (paintings, eco-bijoux)?**

Yes sure! I personally make every single creation in quilling. With the help of a quilling pen and other specific tools, I hand roll each private strip of paper, glue it and pattern it to form various shapes that will eventually comprise a genuinely.

- **I would like a specific style, can I make it in quilling?**

Naturally! Personalized creations are the ones that excite me most! Gather your idea and develop a custom-made creation for yourself based upon your preferences and requirements. In addition to individualized wedding event favors, you can make the best paintings and squares as a wedding event present, birth gift, anniversary present, birthday present, etc.

- **How do I look after my paper quilling jewelry?**

Eco-Bijoux and 3D Objects: these items are protected with water-based paints (non-toxic). Once applied in 2 or 3 layers, the paint will secure the paper, making it resistant to wetness and shocks. To clean a 3D object in Quilling just use a brush with soft bristles. The paint I use (without toxic substances) soaks into the paper, making it stiff, strong and appropriate for daily usage. However it is advised to prevent prolonged contact with water as the paint does not make the paper object completely waterproof. Please do not shower or shower with the jewelry. Just as you would look after any valuable art piece, proper storage of your jewelry and/ or ornaments in a precious jewelry box is recommended and you will extend their life.

- **How do I best protect a painting in Quilling?**

All my paintings are protected by glass or Plexiglas and are intended specifically for indoor environments. They must for that reason be kept in a dry location, safeguarded from heat sources, sources of humidity and direct sunlight.

- **Which frame sizes are suitable for Quilling?**

The size of the frame generally depends upon the quilling design I'm going to make. Given that a quilling work is three-dimensional and has more "height" than pictures or printed works of art, it needs a unique frame, appropriate for consisting of 3d developments. These frames are called "Shadowboxes" (ie deep frames). All frames have a glass or plexiglass security depending on the model selected.

Here are the basic 3D frames you can use:

- Small measurements: external steps 13x18 cm; 19x13 cm

- Typical measurements: external steps 25x25 cm (internal design area: 21x21 cm); 23.7 x23.7 cm (interior design space: 20.5 x20.5); 21x30cm

- Huge size: external measures 30x40 cm (internal style area:-RRB-; 24x43 cm; 30x30 cm.

- Extra big: external dimensions 40x50 cm (internal design space:-RRB-; 40x50 cm; 50x70 cm; 61x91 cm.

- **For how long does it take to develop a custom painting in Quilling?**
Each of the quilling paintings can take from around 4 hours to 20 hours (in some cases a lot more) to make. This depends upon the intricacy and size of the quilling style.

- **Can I make present boxes and customized messages?**
Yes sure! On request, you can get tailored present boxes. I commit a lot of attention and care to the packaging, motivated by the Japanese art of covering "Tsutsumi" according to which, the product packaging is just as important as the present itself, maybe much more.

- **What kind of card should a beginner use?**

Computer printer paper cut into narrow strips (1/8 inch or 3mm) will be fine for practice. When you are ready for real quilling paper, the easiest thing to do is buy it online as you will find a much better selection than in craft stores. The US quilling suppliers are excellent and have American paper brands such as Paplin, Lake City and Quilled Creations, and also the British brand J.J. Quilling designs. The card is pretty cheap, but you may want to join the subscriber list as sales are used occasionally. All are shipped worldwide.

- **I can't understand quilling. How long does it take to learn?**

Because stocks are so simple, quilling is one of those things that people believe should be very easy and straightforward. Roll paper starts to look totally natural after a couple of hours of practice. Not bad for a hobby that could last a lifetime! At first, feeling all the thumbs, I had to keep informing myself that if other people could do it, I could too, it's just paper and glue.

- **Which type of quilling paper works best?**

There are numerous impressive options; solid colors, pearl, metal, parchment, parchment, gold trim and gradient colors are just some of the options. Each type handles slightly differently, but they all roll smoothly. Quilling paper is slightly heavier and softer than computer systems paper. The strips come in various widths ranging from narrow (about 1/16 inch) to 1 inch and most are packaged in multi-colored packaging in addition to individual colors.

- **What quilling tool do you use?**

My favorite tool has an ultra-fine groove, the center crimp sticking out of the groove is barely noticeable. The tool is now available through the Etsy shop.

I use a standard slit tool to make folded roses and when I want coils with round centers without crimping, I use a needle tool. All vendors offer a range of tools; you will surely find one that works for you. Use a stiff wire, my first tool was a muffin tester from my kitchen drawer if you want to get started right away while you wait for your tool to arrive here!

- **What kind of glue do you suggest and how do you apply it?**

My favorite is a clear gel adhesive, as it doesn't create a leathery surface compared to white craft glue. It is odorless and, like quality quilling paper, does not contain acids. My approach to using glue on a reel is to tap on a plastic cap, then pick up an extremely high percentage with the suggestion of a paper piercing tool, cocktail stick, or T-pin. Some prefer to use an ultrafine pointer glue applicator.

• How do you know what size to make loose coils?

I see models that say they use a 3 inch strip wrapped in a loose coil. I have a circular measurement chart, but I don't understand which length strip should go into which hole.

• Are there any standards?

There are no standards. Its three-inch strip can make a slightly different sized coil than another quiller's three-inch strip; it just depends on how hard you roll the paper. The main thing is to roll with tension and your work will have good harmony. The gauge of the rim helps to make the coils of constant size.

• Don't your hands cramp when you put the pen down?

I am happy to say that the answer is no. It can happen if you hold a tool too tightly and / or work for a long time without waiting time. Let's face it, any kind of repeated movement can cause injury. Consciously maintain a relaxed grip on the instrument and periodically extend your hands and fingers. You may want to secure the padding around the tender for maximum comfort. For me it is an enigma why companies do not regularly create all the tools with ergonomically sound management.

• Where can I buy quilling paper for writing?

I can't find quilling paper thicker than regular paper.

Real quilling paper is not as heavy as cardstock, which does not normally roll easily. If you are going to make a curved stripe, the border design (like for the letters) tries cheap cardstock - simply put, very thin.

For the letters, I prefer to use 2 strips of quilling paper glued together. Between the double density and the glue, the paper ends up being quite strong, yet it keeps rolling smoothly. Keep a comfortable damp cloth and slide it down both sides of the strip to remove excess glue as soon as you have attached them. Then, set the strip aside and wait for the glue to dry completely before trying to roll it up.

- **What do you use to cover your finished quilling?**

I don't usually use a fixative because I like the natural look of the paper. Some fasteners produce a glossy plastic finish and application can cause the coil centers to swell. The glass protects it if I made a framed piece. Brushable Liquitex varnish is excellent and is offered in gloss or matte if you are concerned about extreme humidity. Apply an extremely fine pair of coats, never excessive at the same time.

- **How is quilling paper saved?**

There are probably as many answers to this question as there are quillers! The main point to remember is to store the strips in a dry, dust-free place and out of direct sunlight. It is helpful to keep the colors labeled by brand / number in the same clear bags that they come in.

- **How do I mail a quilled card?**

Preferably, you would use a sturdy, shallow box lined with bubble wrap. Instead, place your card between two sheets of cardboard and then in an envelope. If you use an air bubbled bulletin board thinking that it provides enough protection, the paper could wrinkle, so I would include a sheet of cardboard under and on top of the ticket. My Quilling Nest offers innovative advertisements for quilling. The marked cardstock folds easily to form a box. I put a layer of bubble wrap on the front of a card as an added defence.

Conclusion

If you like making cards and crafts, you would surely love to find great paper quilling ideas that you can use in your productions. You can use them in ornaments, to personalize your gifts, cards and scrapbooks, and many other things you can make with them. When expressing your art you can only limit your creativity.

Of course, in art, it is always great to have your own special style in developing your craft so that you can practice and hone your skills and find new things about it. While this is true, it could also help a lot, particularly in quilling, if you can start with some paper quilling ideas from other people who have learned the trade. From there you can work on your design as fast as you explore many other things you can do with quilling.

In any case, we all have to start with the essentials.

You can select the size of the quilling paper based on the design you need to make. The basic paper size you can use is 1/8 ", which you can cut yourself with a paper cutter or shredder, although you may not get this size in a shredder. If you want them to curl perfectly, buy them. Pre - Cut strips are a great alternative. At least you will get a paper of the same size. If you are just starting out, you may also decide to practice cutting paper yourself to save at least a few dollars while still trying your hand on the plane.

To guide you through the correct size of paper you need, if your quilling work involves fine details, you can request narrower strips of quilling paper, such as 1/16 "in size. For 3D sculpting and fringed designs, it is possible you want to use wider strips - 1/2 "or 1/4". For basic projects or when practicing, 1/8 "would be fine.

You can also choose from a range of colors to enhance the style and concepts of your paper quilling. If you choose your card, be sure to choose something that has the exact same color on the front and back of the card, otherwise it will ruin your surface product. Lightweight cardstock will work just fine.

Glue selection is also important in making your art. Of course, you don't want your pen style to be smeared with visible white glue everywhere. It is recommended that you select a clear dry glue to avoid ruining your art. One method to help you glue your particular creations, including those big curls, is to spread the glue on a piece of paper and with tweezers, you can gently press down on your feathered styles just enough so that the bottom has enough glue. to your album or card. You can also use toothpicks to help it stick.

You can then create your own design and squeeze your innovative juices to create designs that don't exist yet if you master the fundamentals. This will really set your imagination free and allow you to create your own style. If you want to learn more paper quilling ideas and master the art of quilling, you must first figure out how to make standard designs and shapes. You can discover helpful resources that will teach you step-by-step how to transform teardrop styles into square styles and other patterns. In the same way it will work to observe the quilling masters and win with them.

Thank you for reading this book.

If you enjoyed it, please visit the site where you purchased it and write a brief review. Your feedback is important to me and will help other readers decide whether to read the book too.

Thank you!

Brenda Sanders